VISITOR'S GUIDE

—TO—

NEW ORLEANS.

NOVEMBER, 1875.

PUBLISHED BY

J. CURTIS WALDO,

Southern Publishing & Advertising House

No. 56 CAMP STREET,

(OVER GAUTHREAUX & WRIGHT'S),

NEW ORLEANS, LA.

INDEX.

To the Memory

OF THE LATE

William Stephen Pike,

whose long life of usefulness in our midst, marked by countless acts of charity, and unwavering devotion to the best interests of our city and State, have endeared his name to the people of New Orleans, this work is most respectfully inscribed,

J. CURTIS WALDO.

1875	Sun	Mon	Tue	Wed	Thu	Fri	Sat
Nov.	...	1	2	3	4	5	6
	7	8	9	10	11	12	13
	14	15	16	17	18	19	20
	21	22	23	24	25	26	27
	28	29	30	...	...	...	...
Dec.	...	...	...	1	2	3	4
	5	6	7	8	9	10	11
	12	13	14	15	16	17	18
1876	19	20	21	22	23	24	25
	26	27	28	29	30	31	...
	...	...	...	...	...	...	...
Jan.	...	...	...	...	...	...	1
	2	3	4	5	6	7	8
	9	10	11	12	13	14	15
	16	17	18	19	20	21	22
	23	24	25	26	27	28	29
	30	31	...	...	...	...	...
Feb.	...	...	1	2	3	4	5
	6	7	8	9	10	11	12
	13	14	15	16	17	18	19
	20	21	22	23	24	25	26
	27	28	29	...	...	...	...
Mar.	...	...	...	1	2	3	4
	5	6	7	8	9	10	11
	12	13	14	15	16	17	18
	19	20	21	22	23	24	25
	26	27	28	29	30	31	...
Apr.	...	...	...	...	...	...	1
	2	3	4	5	6	7	8
	9	10	11	12	13	14	15
	16	17	18	19	20	21	22
	23	24	25	26	27	28	29
	30	...	...	...	...	...	...
May.	...	1	2	3	4	5	6
	7	8	9	10	11	12	13
	14	15	16	17	18	19	20
	21	22	23	24	25	26	27
	28	29	30	31	...	...	...

1876	Sun	Mon	Tue	Wed	Thu	Fri	Sat
June	...	...	...	...	1	2	3
	4	5	6	7	8	9	10
	11	12	13	14	15	16	17
	18	19	20	21	22	23	24
	25	26	27	28	29	30	...
July	...	...	...	...	...	...	1
	2	3	4	5	6	7	8
	9	10	11	12	13	14	15
	16	17	18	19	20	21	22
	23	24	25	26	27	28	29
	30	31	...	...	...	...	...
Aug.	...	...	1	2	3	4	5
	6	7	8	9	10	11	12
	13	14	15	16	17	18	19
	20	21	22	23	24	25	26
	27	28	29	30	31	...	...
Sept	...	...	...	...	...	1	2
	3	4	5	6	7	8	9
	10	11	12	13	14	15	16
	17	18	19	20	21	22	23
	24	25	26	27	28	29	30
Oct.	...	...	...	...	...	...	...
	1	2	3	4	5	6	7
	8	9	10	11	12	13	14
	15	16	17	18	19	20	21
	22	23	24	25	26	27	28
	29	30	31	...	...	...	...
Nov.	...	...	...	1	2	3	4
	5	6	7	8	9	10	11
	12	13	14	15	16	17	18
	19	20	21	22	23	24	25
	26	27	28	29	30	...	...
Dec.	...	...	...	...	...	1	2
	3	4	5	6	7	8	9
	10	11	12	13	14	15	16
	17	18	19	20	21	22	23
	21	25	26	27	28	29	30
	31	...	...	...	...	...	...

INTRODUCTION.

We are indebted to H. N. Jenkins, Esq, the well known Agent for patents, Col. J. F. H. Claiborne, Major W. M. Robinson, News-Editor of the Republican, and other friends who have kindly placed at our disposal, many books and papers relating to the early history of our city.

From these we have endeavored to collate such facts as we believed would be most interesting to our readers, but we are mainly indebted for these data, to Gibson's Guide and Directory of New Orleans, published in 1838, and to the Directory issued in 1823 by John Adems Paxton, who published in 1822, the first directory ever compiled in this city, courteously loaned to us by a lady, Mrs. E. M.

This is an age of work and activity, when the majority of men demand facts in short sentences; and we have endeavored to tell our story, so that those "who run may read."

The historian who has the facts and figures of the early days of New Orleans at his tongue's end, and the antiquarian who has delved among ancient books and papers until he can tell the original owner of nearly every lot of ground in our city, will find little that is new in our Glance at the Past, but even these, will find some interesting reading among the descriptions of objects belonging to our own time.

We expect criticism, and when found, shall "make a note of it;" we shall take advice kindly, and try to benefit by all suggestions thrown out for our guidance in a second number of the "Visitor's Guide," which we trust a generous and interested public may demand.

A GLANCE AT THE PAST.

The first attempt of the French to install a colony in Louisiana, was made by the brave and chivalrous La Salle, who left France with all requisite for the establishment of a settlement, but the expedition was wrecked in the Gulf of Mexico, and the leader, after escaping with a few of his followers, was murdered by them for some fancied wrong.

Iberville, very justly termed the father of Louisiana, arrived at Cat Island in 1698, and soon afterwards a settlement was made at the now favorite Lake Shore summer resort, Biloxi.

Souville was appointed the first Governor, and Bienville Lieutenant Governor. In 1701 Souville died, and was succeeded by Bienville, who retained the chief office until 1710, when he was removed and De Muys and the Baron D'Artaquette assumed the charge of the destinies of the young colony.

The settlement at Biloxi was surrounded with many difficulties and perils, and although frequently aided by supplies, and strengthened with new emigrants from France, did not prosper.

In 1717 the famous company, of which the Scotch financier, Law was the ruling spirit, was formed, and received from the King of France, Louis Fourteenth, extraordinary and absolute power in the new colony.

In 1718 Bienville was re-appointed Governor, and, his first act was to seek a more suitable locality for the chief settlement of the province. Sailing along Lake Pontchartrain, just as night was overtaking his Company, the Governor discovered a small stream leading inwards, and proceeding up this water until he found a high place, suitable for a camp, he halted and built his fires for the night, near where now stand the boat houses of the St. John and Pelican Rowing Clubs, at Bayou Bridge, on the

Bayou St. John, the name given to the small stream he had been ascending.

And thus the first step towards the foundation of the new city, whose commerce in the future should extend to the utmost limits of the globe, and whose people should rival in beauty, fashion and chivalry, Paris itself, was made on the spot where, in our day, the "fairest of the fair" gather to witness the strength and swiftness of the Knights of the Oar, and miriads of lights at night, on festal occasions, play on the waters, where first were mirrowed the beacon fires of the future Queen of the South, the beautiful New Orleans, so named after the Duke of Orleans. Bienville left fifty men to clear the ground and erect the necessary buildings, which for the better commerce of the province were placed on the banks of the Mississippi.

The first overflow that we find recorded, occured in 1719, one year after the settlement was planned. The river rose to an extraordinary height, and, as the Company was as yet unable to protect themselves by dykes, the place was for a time deserted.

The principal offices and establishments of the province were removed from Biloxi to New Orleans, in November, 1722. In the following year, we are told by Charlevoix, who came from Canada by way of the river, that the city then consisted of one hundred cabins, very irregularly placed, a large wooden warehouse, two or three dwellings, a poor store-house, which was also used as a chapel, a shed being converted into the house of prayer. The population did not exceed two hundred persons.

Historians mention as an important fact, that in this year, 1723, a party of emigrants from Germany, who had crossed the ocean to settle on lands in Arkansas, granted to them by the celebrated Law, being disappointed in their original intention, descended the river to New Orleans, hoping to obtain a passage back to France. This the government was unable to furnish, but small tracts of land were given to them on both sides of the river about thirty miles above New Orleans, at what is known as the German Coast, where they settled and engaged in agricultural pursuits, supplying the city with vegetables and garden products. This was the commencement of the German element in the population of our city, and the decendants of these early settlers augmented by thousands of others from the Fatherland, make one of the most industrious, reliable, prosperous and honorable classes of our miscellaneous community. In the fall of this year the town was visited by a terrific cyclone, which swept before it the church, hospital, and about one third of the residences of the inhabitants. This disaster which was also very destructive to the crops, seriously inclined many of the people to abandon the settlement.

The Jesuit Fathers first arrived in the summer of 1727, and located on a tract of land in the Faubourg St. Mary, now known as the First District, in which they made great improvements—erecting imposing and valuable buildings.

The Ursuline Nuns also came to the city in this year, and first lived in a house corner of Bienville and Chartres streets. In 1730 they removed to their convent corner of Conde, now Chartres, and Ursulines streets. This building was occupied by them, with the large grounds around it, about three squares in size, for nearly a century, The growth of the city and consequent rise in real estate, made this property very valuable, and the Nuns disposed of the greater part of it, and erected their new convent near where the Barracks now stands, and removed to it in 1824.

In 1728 the city extended from Customhouse street to Barrack street, and from the river to Claiborne street. It was very regularly laid out, but the houses were scattered and few. The inhabitants probably had no more idea that their little settlement would one day be a city of the magnitude and importance of the New Orleans of to-day, than we have of the enterprise, wealth and power our city will hold twenty-five or even ten years hence.

In 1763 the Jesuits were compelled to leave Louisiana, they having been expelled, by a decree of Clement 13th, from the dominions of the Kings of France, Spain and Naples. Their property in New Orleans was seized and sold for about one hundred and eighty thousand dollars —property which to-day is worth many millions, embracing as it did, by far the most valuable portion of the First District.

Commerce with Great Britian began in 1764, during which year the first British vessels visited the Mississippi. Coming up the river they would make fast to a tree opposite the now beautiful and flourishing Fourth District and there carry on a profitable trafic with the citizens and inhabitants of the neighbood.

In the year 1769, the colony of Louisiana was, much against the wishes of the colonists, ceded to Spain, and the capital was taken possession of by General Alexander O'Reilly, one of the most distingushed officers of the Spanish army. The transfer of the colony was attended with great pomp and show of power, General O'Reilly being accompanied by a large force, for the purpose of overawing those who had joined in the insurrection during the preceding year against the authority of Spain.

The first appearance of that much dreaded disease, Yellow Fever, was in the summer of this year. It was imported, as all authorities agree, in a British vessel, which arrived from the coast of Africa, with a cargo of slaves. Although the city has since been visited by many terrible epidemics of this scourge, it is not regarded by our native citizens or those who have lived here long enough to become acquainted with the true nature of the disease, with that dread usually entertained for it by strangers. In fact it has often been observed that its ravages have been principally among those who either could not, or would not take proper care of themselves. Our experienced nurses generally regard it with less apprehension than many diseases prevelent in other sections of the Union.

In the year of 1770 the city was visited by an intensely cold spell, during which the river was frozen for several yards on both sides, the only instance of the kind that we find recorded.

The population of New Orleans steadily increased from this time forward although very slowly at first. In 1770 the city had 3190 residents and in 1785, 4980, exclusive of the surrounding settlements.

The commerce of the place was greatly retarded for several years by the restrictions and onerous exactions of the Spanish authorities, but a more liberal policy having been inaugurated in 1778, the drooping fortunes of the place revived.

In 1785 the Americans began the trade from the West to New Orleans, which has ever since been an important element in the industries of the place. About the same time many merchants came from France and established themselves here. British vessels navigated the Mississippi, trading with the citizens and planters, taking produce in payment for their merchandise or giving long credits, and at this period, the Philadelphians opened a brisk business with this city.

On Good Friday of 1788 a very destructive conflagation occurred. It commenced in the chapel of a Spaniard on Chartres street, about three o'clock in the afternoon, and it being a very boisterous and windy day, about nine hundred houses were destroyed before the flames could be subdued. The loss in money was estimated at two and a half million dollars. The citizens of our day, protected by a gallant corps of men, organized into one of the most effective Fire Departments ever known to the world, and amply supplied with steam fire engines, and Babcock Extinguishers, read of such desolation with astonishment.

It was in 1788 that General Wilkinson first procured permission to send launches from Kentucky loaded with tobacco, thus opening trade in an article for which New Orleans has since become a leading mart.

The first settlements of Americans that we find mentioned took place in 1789, and their numbers and influence have grown with each year since.

The first company of French comedians arrived in New Orleans in 1791, having escaped from a revolt of the slaves at Cape François.

The Baron Carondelet arrived in 1792 and took charge of the colony as Governor. He at once took measures for the improvement of the city, among which were lighting the streets and the employment of watchmen.

The revenues of the city, which then amounted to about

seven thousand dollars per annum, not being sufficient to pay these expenses, a tax of one dollar and twelve and a half cents was laid on each chimney. Baron Carondelet erected new fortifications; a fort was constructed below the city on the site of the present U. S. Mint, and another at the upper confines, foot of Canal street, and a strong redoubt at each angle of the city, and on Rampart street. He also opened a canal to connect the city with Lake Pontchartrain by way of Bayou St John. This was completed in 1795 and has always been known as Canal Carondelet.

He likewise caused the militia to be trained. There were at the time five companies of volunteers, one of artillery and two of riflemen, each of one hundred men.

The first newspaper ever published in this city was commenced in 1794 and was called "Le Moniteur de la Louisiane," (The Louisiana Monitor)

Evan Jones, the first consul of the United States was delegated in 1799, the commerce with the Republic having become sufficiently important, at that date, to induce the President to make the appointment.

On the 21st March, 1801, Louisiana was ceded to the French Republic, and in the same year Daniel Clark was appointed Consul of the United States. He was the father of that courageous and persevering woman Mrs. Myra Clark Gaines, whose indefatigable efforts to establish her claims to the property of her father have made her a national fame.

Napoleon, as First Consul of France ceded the province of Louisiana to the United States on the 30th of April 1803, and formal possession was taken on the 30th of November following, just seventy two years ago.

What momentous changes have taken place in that short time. The population of the city was not quite 8100, while that of all of what is now known as Louisiana was but 42000. The receipts of the CustomHouse for 1802 amounted to $117,515, and the revenues of the city only $19,278,

The annual produce of the entire province was estimated at 300lbs. indigo; 20,000 bales cotton, of 300lbs. each; 5000 hogsheads of sugar, and 5000 casks of molasses.

Naturally enough the transfer to the United States caused great dissatisfaction with the people of the province, but American energy and enterprise soon gave new life to the place. New coinage and modes of business were introduced, the judiciary was remodeled and the general machinery of the government completely changed. The restless and progressive spirit of Americans has made great innovations on the manners and customs of the place, and although the old peculiarities of the French yet remain to some degree, in the lower part of the city, they are fast disappearing before the aggressive energy of our age.

The first officers of the city under the change, were Boré, Mayor, with whom were associated Destrehan and Sauve. The council was composed of Livaudais, Petit Cavelier, Villeré, Jones, Fortier, Donaldson, Faurie, Alard, Tureaud, and Watkins Derbigny was Secretary and Labatut, Treasurer.

In 1804, the city of New Orleans was made a port of entry and delivery, and the Bayou St John a port of delivery.

New Orleans was first incorporated as a city by the Legislative Council of the Territory, in 1805 and the officers were Mayor, Recorder, Fourteen Aldermen and one Treasurer. A branch of the United States Bank was this year established in New Orleans.

Under the new administration of affairs, the population of the city trebled in seven years, and in 1810 amounted to 24,552.

At that time, what is now known as the First District, in which is located the finest buildings and the most extensive stores and warehouses of the city, was mostly used as a plantation It was the property of a wealthy citizen named Gravier, and one of our principal streets running through this District now bears his name.

With the exception of here and there a villa on the levee, the city extended no further down than Esplanade street, nor above Canal street, except an occasional house.

There were a few dwellings on Canal and Magazine streets and the Polar Star Lodge, situated at the corner of Camp and Gravier streets was considered as being in the country. There were no paved streets in the city, and when some time later, the first attempt at such an improvement was made by V. Rillieux and Benjamin Morgan, they were looked upon as dreaming speculators.

The first steamboat—The New Orleans—that ever made the passage of the Mississippi River, landed at our wharf on the 10th of January 1812, having made the trip in 229 hours, from Fort du Quesne, now Pittsburg. Her presence aroused an immense enthusiasm, for already the success of the experiment had been demonstrated, and it was looked to as the greatest agent for the development of the country. This pioneer steam vessel, was soon followed by fleets of steamers, giving increased facilities and cheap rates for the transportation of passengers and freights, inducing an immense emigation from the older States and Europe, developing the unbounded resources of the great West and South,

This craft, which excited vast interest in New Orleans, was nothing in comparison to the present day floating palaces on our rivers, and wonderful creations of mechanical genius and superior intelligence, yet in proportion to the experiments of that relic of the past, there is nothing we know of, fraught with so much interest to the human welfare of the age. Its successful trip inaugurated all the vast machinery and tremendous appliances that make the rich and fertile West populous, and ever steadily progress in the march of improvement and greatness. In it was the germ of a colossal enterprise, that has developed all the utilitarian greatness of this wonderful century of incomparable excellence in mechanical arts and contrivances. We wonder now if the perfection of human genius has culminated, as much as those astonished people did when they saw the first steamer.

General Andrew Jackson arrived in New Orleans, December 1st, 1812, and immediately began preparation for the defense of the city. On the 8th of January the famous battle of New Orleans was fought, culminating in a victory which gave undying glory to the name of the sturdy old hero. On the 23d of January 1815, the success of the Americans was solemnized by a period of Thanksgiving in the Cathedral. The most gorgeous and impressive ceremonies of the church, added to the grand military display, made the occasion one of the most memorable celebrations ever known in New Orleans.

General Lafayette visited New Orleans in 1825. The demonstrations of welcome and kindly gratitude expressed by the people to the famous patriot and soldier, who generously espoused the cause of our Country in its severest moment of trial, were of the most brilliant character, and fully in consonance with the princely hospitality and refined culture of the brave and generous people of this section.

In 1828, General Jackson made a short stay in our city, and was the recipient of the most lavish attention from citizens of all classes—every one striving to do him honor. The old hero revisited the field of Chalmette, rendered famous in song and story by his own skill and the bravery of his troops. His visit was one grand ovation, alike due to his high merit as a soldier and statesman, and the people's own feelings of love and gratitude.

New Orleans owes much to the energy, courage and perseverance of James H. Caldwell, whose name for a long period of years was connected with every enterprise for the advancement and improvement of the place.

In 1823-4 Mr. Caldwell erected the American Theatre, in Camp street, which was for a long time approachable only over flat-boat Gunwales. This building was subsequently known as the Armory Hall, and is still in a good state of preservation, being at the present time in use as an auction mart. Mr. Caldwell's venture was regarded as a very ridiculous move, but others followed his example, and the immediate neighborhood of his theatre soon became the most prosperous part of the city.

Speaking of this improvement, and the upward growth of the city, Norman in his Guide Book issued in 1845, relates the following anecdote :

"Some of the old Frenchmen in the city proper, who have rarely trusted themselves three squares beyond their favorite cabaret, are very incredulous of the reported progress and improvement in the Faubourg St. Mary. A few years since, a gentleman of the second municipality, asked the old cabaret keeper, who has made himself illustrious and wealthy by vending to the habitues of the lower market, a drink of his own compounding, called "*Pig and Whistle*," why he did not come up into the

Faubourg St. Mary, and see the buildings? At the same time describing the St. Charles Exchange, the Theatre, the Verandah, Bank's Arcade, the magnificent stores, etc. The old Frenchman listened in doubting wonder for some time, at last however, his faith and his gravity both gave way and he burst into a laugh, exclaiming "Oh monsieur B. dat is too much! You von varry funny fellow—I no believ vat you say—its only von grand—vat you call it—vere de mud, de aligator, and de bull frog live. Von grand—grand—mud swamp, vere you say is one grand city, I no believ it!"

Gas was introduced into New Orleans by Mr. Caldwell in 1834, he having lighted his theatre with it several years previous. The works are, we believe, the best arranged in the United States.

The growth of the city progressed favorably for many years, but little of interest occuring, beyond the gradual widening of the limits of "brick and mortar," the increase in our imports and exports and the consequent additional wealth of our citizens. The fearful panic of 1837 exerted for a time a baleful influence, but recovering from this, enterprise and prosperity went hand in hand again.

The writer arrived in New Orleans on the 3d of December 1847, a date indelibly fixed in his mind from the fact, that on the day following, General Zachary Taylor, arrived in the city, on his return from Mexico, and was received with grand military and civic honors, the procession which escorted him being one of the most imposing parades ever witnessed here.

On the evening of Feburry 24, 1857 (Mardi Gras) the Mistick Krewe of Comus made their first appearance on the streets of New Orleans, Their brilliant pageants which have followed every year since, except 1862, 1863, 1864, and 1865, when the fierce spirit of war stalked through the land, and last year, which was marked by threatning political troubles, have made them a world wide fame. We have heard from the best authority, that Comus will marshal his merry krewe on the coming Mardi Gras. Febuary 29th 1876, and present to our citizens and visitors a display which in taste and magnificence will rival any of his former efforts.

To record the various incidents which occurred in our city during the "Great Struggle" or the misfortunes which have followed in its wake we do not think within our province. The history of those events can not now be written by the one side, nor read by the other with interest or profit. In the time to come some more gifted pen will weave the garland of fame, due to the heroism, bravery and endurence of Louisiana's Soldiers, a just tribute to the patience, fortitude and forbearance of her citizens, through the wrongs and outrages heaped upon them under the guise of law, since the surrender of the armies of the South. Impressively eloquent are the voiceless memories that come to us from the glorious past. The sons of New Orleans have stood in the front of every well contested field of battle, with a courage and daring that challenged the admiration of both friends and foes, and at the downfall of the cause they loved so well, resumed their peaceful avocations, accepting the verdict of fate, with a resignation and truth to their plighted faith, no less honorable than their record on the blood stained field of war.

THE PRESENT

Presuming that many copies of this work will find their way abroad, and consequently into the hands of those who do not know our city, we shall make no excuse for entering into some details which to those who are "native and to the manor born" will be an "oft told tale"

New Orleans is situated on the left bank of the Mississippi River, one hundred and five miles from its mouth, about 1200 miles below St. Louis, 1000 miles distant from Cairo, and 1203 miles south-west of Washington city. The city is built on a plain which slopes gently from the river to Lake Pontchartrain, and although the improvements do not now extend more than half that distance, the corporate limits embrace the whole territory to the shores of the lake, and when the present admirable system of drainage shall have been perfected, all of this ground will, without doubt, be occupied. The curve in the river around which the city is built, gives it the poetical name of Cresent City, while it derives its now common title of New Orleans, from the compliment paid by its founders,to the Duke of Orleans, then Regent of France.

By recent annexations the municipal authority has been extended, so that the late towns of Algiers, Jefferson City and Carrollton, are now embraced under the name of New Orleans, and are known respectively as the Fifth, Sixth and Seventh districts. This gives us room, not only for improvement, but for additional workers. The present population of New Orleans is not far from 280,000, and is made up of, perhaps, a greater admixture of races than can be found in any other city in the world. Originally laid out by the French and subsequently transferred to the Spanish, it is natural that there should be a strong element of the Latin races in our population.

These still preserve in a great degree the characteristics of the mother country. They are chivalrous, brave, warm hearted and generous.

The old time German families—descendents of the deluded emigrants, noticed in our opening article, with constant additions from the Father-land make another strong element in the population of New Orleans. They, like their fathers, are hard working, cautions and saving, and consequently control much of the wealth of the city. We have also a very noticeable Irish class, as impulsive, brave and generous as their ancestors, whose valor, learning and refinement, made Ireland the home of saints, sages and soldiers for so many ages.

Next comes the American element, the hardy and enterprising men from the Western and Middle States, and the shrewd, calculating Yankee, who, in less than a century, have by peaceful means captured the city, and may now be said to hold in their hands the destiny of the Southern metropolis. They lead the way in energy, enterprise and improvement, and cordially striking hands with their fellow citizens of more ancient residence and lineage, point out the road to future wealth and power for the section dear to all.

Speaking of the people of Louisiana, a celebrated historian says "There were but humble dwellings in Louisiana, in 1769, and he who would have judged of their tenants from their outward appearance, would have thought that they were occupied by mere peasants, but had he passed their thresholds, he would have been amazed at being welcomed with such manners as were habitual in the most polished Courts of Europe, and entertained by men and women, wearing with the utmost ease and grace, the elegant and rich costumes of the reign of Louis XV."

In this respect New Orleans is "true to her ancient fame;"—her people are sociable, friendly and hospitable, and through every class of society there extends a courteous, refined and dignified manner, which to the stranger is marked indeed. Few who come here to live but soon acknowledge the sway of these feelings; even the rough and most uncouth, the most energetic and grasping are in time "toned down" until they seem, at least, to possess the characteristics of the polite Southern.

Although we can not claim for our city the architectural beauty which distinguishes her more northern sisters, our stores are large and commodious, and admirably adapted to the uses of commerce, and our residences are convenient, well ventilated and comfortable, and generally surrounded with gardens in which the rarest flowers fill the air with perpetual fragrance.

New Orleans has been much maligned in relation to its health and salubrity. No city in the United States enjoys a better climate, the heat is not so excessive nor the cold so intense as in other places of the same latitude. It is acknowledged in fact, by those who have lived in more Northern cities, that ours is the most enjoyable climate they have ever proved. Many who have dreaded a summer here, after once experiencing that season with its cool nights and pleasant afternoons, prefer it to any other part of the year. Our bill of health will compare favorably that with of any large city in the country.

The dreaded Yellow Fever, is yearly becoming less virulent; the last great epidimic having occurred in 1853 and the proportions of recoveries in excess of deaths has been greater in each subsequent visitation of the disease. The process of acclimating is in fact regraded with very little fear, and to those who act prudently is really accompanied with very little danger. Natives and acclimated citizens enjoy as good health and attain as great an age, as the people of any part of the world.

Pulminary complaints are rarely known as originating here, the deaths from these causes are principally of parties who have contracted the disease in other parts.

New Orleans by its position commands a vast commercial importance. The Mississippi river and its branches have over twenty thousand miles of navigable streams, which drain 1,226,600 square miles, embracing the most fertile lands of the earth, on which every variety of crops may be grown and for which the natural and cheapest outlet to the markets of the world is the great Father of Waters, making New Orleans the central depot for the produce, brought from more than a thousand rivers.

With the rapidly developing States of Florida, Alabama, Mississippi, and Arkansas, almost surrounding us, Cuba in front, Mexico and the giant State of Texas on the right, and the great valley of the Mississippi to the North and

West, no such po ition for gathering of wealth and power ever existed.

It needs not the mantle of a prophet to predict the future prosperity, and magnificence of New Orleans. With the developement of the immense region, for which she is the natural mart, a region capable of supporting more than one hundred millions of industrious and intelligent people, the business must come. It matters not that rivals have for the time diverted a portion of her trade, that her citizens, benummed by the disasters of civil war and the distruction of hundreds of millions of property, have for years seemed to labor against hope.

With intelligence and refinement, our people combine sagacity, fortitude and indomitable perseverance; although misfortunes have for a time over-clouded their spirits, it needs but a breath of returning prosperity to renew their energies, and make them the most active, courageous and successful citizens of this great republic.

In the early history of Louisiana, then embracing Florida, Arkansas, Missouri and the territories of the far West, New Orleans was selected as the capitol; after passing through the severest trials, from epidemics floods and war, she appears to be again emerging into prosperity, and if her natural advantages are properly backed by the ambition, energy and perseverance of her citizens, the near future will again witness her as, at least, the commercial metropolis of all that broad area once known as Louisiana.

PUBLIC SQUARES.

When the "city proper was bounded by the spacious streets, Canal, Rampart, Esplanade and Champs Elysées, 1320 yards along the river and 700 wide backwards towards the swamp," we are told that there were "several large public squares, one of which, the Place of Arms, 350 feet on the Levee, by 330 in depth to Chartres Street, is very handsome, being planted with trees, and enclosed with an iron palisade, having beautiful ornamental gateways of the same metal. The expenses of fi ting this place up, amount to $26,000."

This was in 1823, over half a century ago, when the city's limits were insignificant as above stated; when the yearly revenue, from all sources amounted to but $130,000, a population of 29,000 including whites and blacks, slaves and free, and. "in the whole 8705 houses of every description." Now in the year of our Lord 1875, when New Orleans has a river front of nearly twelve miles and a width of six and a half; when her revenues are counted by the million, and her population by hundred of thousands; in speaking of our Public Squares, we can say little more than was said by John Adems Paxton, fifty two years ago: for although several beautiful localities have been set apart from time to time as "Public Squares for the pleasure of the people, and to beautify the city," with the exception of fencing in, and the planting of a few trees the majority of these places presents very scanty improvements, no attempts whatever in the beautifying line, and are standing reproaches to "all whom it may concern." Yet as Nature has done so much that man neglected to do, and as most of the public squares have beautiful surroundings, and many of them an interesting history, an inspection of them will well repay the visitor.

JACKSON SQUARE.

This beautiful pleasure ground which is bounded by Chartres, Decatur or Old Levee, St. Anne and St. Peter Streets is the oldest public square in New Orleans, and is interesting as well on account of its appearance as of its historical surroundings. This square was formerly called the PLACE D'ARMS, but being selected as the site of the statue of General Jackson, the old veteran's name was bestowed on it, while its former cognomen was transferred to another of our ancient parks.

The splendid rows of the Pontalba building, with their inposing fronts and broad verandas, overlook the square from the North and South, the Cathedral and Court Houses on the West, while the mighty Father of Waters, may be seen on the East. A massive paling of iron set in granite encloses this peculiar square, which is European in design, and almost purely tropical in productions.

The bronze equestrian statue of "Old Hickory," the most conspicuous object in the square, stands in the center, on ground slightly elevated, based on an enormous block of granite, and protected by a tasteful iron railing. The statue represents the stern old hero in the full dress uniform of his day, lifting his military hat in salute, his ponderous sword hanging from his belt and his left hand grasping the reins of his war steed. The horse is represented in the act of rearing, and stands balanced on his hind legs. It is a faithful and spirited copy from life, and reflects the highest credit on the artist who designed it, and the workers who carried out his intentions.

Diverging from the statue in all directions, are beautifully graded walks, bordered with the choicest flowers of the South, luxurient vines and evergreens, which at all seasons of the year present a pleasing picture to the eye. Magnificent orange trees with their golden wealth of fruit in autumn, stately magnolias, clustering bananas under their shade of gigantic leaves, birds of rare plumage, the notes of the mocking bird mingling with the merry voices of happy children, the tread of pedestrians, the rattle of cars and carriages, the sonorous breathing of steamers, and the warning echoes of the old cathedral clock, whose strokes have sounded in the ears of generations forever passed away, render this one of the most interesting places in the "land of sun and flowers."

The historical reminiscences of the "old square," would of themselves make a large volume, while the tender romances, begun, matured or consumated under the favoring shade of its trees, would form more thrilling tales than were ever conceived in the brain of the most vivid writer of fiction. Languishing Spanish beauties, piquant French belles, sweet faced daughters from classic Italy or storied Greece, the women of every clime, have in this spot listened to the witching tale they love to hear, Soldiers have been drilled, arms stacked or distributed to the defenders of their "ain" fireside, in fact all the phases of human joy or woe, honor or disgrace, hope or fear, have been enacted and experienced in the old Jackson Square.

PLACE D'ARMS.

The place which now bears this name, but better known

as "Congo Square," is a large and pleasantly situated prominade ground, between Rampart, St. Claude, St. Peter, and St. Anne streets. It was in "old times" called the "Circus Public Square" and was then noted as the place, "where the Congo and other negroes *dance, carouse* and debauch on the Sabbath, to the great injury of the rising generation. It is a foolish custom that elicits the ridicule of most respectable persons who visit the city."

The "foolish custom" had been numbered among the things of the past long before the war, but there are many in our midst who recall the time, and with pleasure too, when they went "to see the negroes dance," and who are still inclied to the belief that they were "good old times," and that the visitors who were scandalized, were of the number who could not descern the "beam in their own eye" but were painfully conscious of the mote in their neighbors.

Esplanade and Rampart street cars pass this ancient place of rendezvous.

LAFAYETTE SQUARE.

Is considered by many the handsomest in the First District, and has two of the most prominent streets, Camp and St. Charles in its front and rear, and several of our finest public buildings in its immediate vicinity.

It is enclosed by an iron railing, is well laid off in broad regular walks, and has a great many beautiful well grown trees, beneath which the seeker of ease may recline in the shade, at any hour of even the most sunny day. Here is placed a statue of the philosopher, Benjamin Franklin, in white marble, executed by the famous Hiram Power, which was presented to the city by that public spirited, liberal gentleman, Mr. Charles A. Weed, formerly proprietor of the New Orleans *Times*,

ANNUNICATION SQUARE.

This, the largest and among the best situated public squares of the city is in the upper part of the First District, and may in some future day be improved, as no doubt was the original intention. Orange and Race streets bound it North and South, and facing it are many very beautiful private residences, and St. Michael (Catholic) Church and school house.

NEW CITY PARK.

Some years ago the city purchased a track of land, containing two hundred and sixty-five acres situated almost six squares above Nashville Avenue and extending from St. Charles street to the river bank. It is splendidly located for an up town park but as yet no steps have been taken towards its improvement.

DOUGLASS SQUARE.

Was enclosed in 1864, and was tastefully laid out, well planted, and cared for during a few years. It is now rich in an irregular luxurient growth of trees, shrubs and flowers. It is bounded by Washington Avenue, George, Second, and Freret Streets.

THE CITY PARK.

Over twenty years ago the late John McDonough bequeathed to the city for a Public Park, a track of ground containing an area of about half of a square mile, fronting on the Metaire Road, between the old and new canals. The ground is high and well adapted to the purpose for which it was intended. It is famous for the Live-oak trees that grow within its limits, some of which spread out their branches on all sides to an incredable extent, and give a dense shade. No attempts have yet been made to lay out or adorn the Park, but, as the city is spreading fast in that direction, it is presumable that work will be commenced on it within a few years.

Its numerous natural advantages as a pleasure ground make it a favorite resort for Pic Nics and other sociable excursions, and in the season suited to such entertainments, hundreds of merry revelers may be seen seated or dancing under the grand old oaks, or strolling through the woods in quest of the flowers and wonderful ferns with which the place abounds,

The other Public Squares, Tivole Circle, Coliseum Place, Clay, Washington, and Lawrence present no noticable features.

DRIVES.

We have no lofty mountains, towering in majestic proportions to the skies, no vales lingering between snow capped hills, no musical streams meandering over rocks and cliffs to the ever surging sea. But we have broad savannas and fertile plains bearing the richest wealth of the world, on these are the most exquisite foliage and most beautiful flowers of the earth, enriching the air with their perfume. The sweetest zephyrs float gently through the leaves bringing calm delight to all true lovers of the beautiful in nature.

The favorite drive for the majority of visitors is on the

SHELL ROAD

to the New Lake End. Procuring a vehicle suitable to our taste, we drive out Canal street, take in either side as far as Claiborne, where we take the right hand side of the broad neutral ground, and are immediately on the shell road. This road is as level and well kept as the track of a race course, and for those who wish to "make good time," presents special attractions.

Lining both sides of the road as far as the Metaire Ridge there are residences, many of them surrounded by beautiful gardens. At the Metarie Ridge will be found St. Patricks, Odd Fellows Rest, Cypress Grove, Greenwood, Metaire and other cemeteries, all of them objects of interest, and containing many tombs well worthy of a visit. As we turn from Canal street to cross the bridge on the New Canal we will see in Greenwood cemetery, the beautiful monument erected by the ladies of New Orleans to the memory of the Confederate dead.

Across the canal is the Half-Way House where refreshments may be obtained, and the garden of which is one of the finest in Southern country.

Resuming the road we will go down the banks of the

canal, richly foliaged trees lining the left, which throw a delightful shade on the way, and are mirrored in varying shades and fantastic shapes in the limped waters of the stream. From the Half Way house to the lake the road is kept in splendid condition by the Canal Company, who levy a toll of twenty-five cents on all vehicles passing down, at the lake end we can stop at either of the three hotels for a fine dinner, which will be served in supurb style and may be flanked by as fine wines as can be found on this side of the Atlantic. We can now drive over the bridge, out on to the new protection levee, and along its summit, giving a delightful evening view of the placid waters of Lake Pontchartrain, and as glorious a sun-set as ever was witnessed. The return may be made by the road on the banks of the canal, or by following the protection levee to its end, and taking the road in the rear, lately put in excellent order, coming back to the canal at the Half-Way House. Another enjoyable drive is by

WASHINGTON AVENUE.

Going up St. Charles street, passing Tivoli circle, and some of the most palatial residences of the city. We will find this part of the road delightful and interesting. Upon reaching Washington avenue, a wide, smooth street covered with shells, well rolled down, we turn to the right, and follow the road by which we will come out upon the New Canal, at a point about six blocks above the Half-Way house. On the way down we will pass Douglas Square, and several of our best laid out cemeteries. The ground is high partly shaded, and a cool breeze will nearly always be found blowing from the lake. After reaching the New Canal we may proceed by the shell road to the lake or crossing the bridge at Half-Way house return to the city by the Canal Street road already mentioned.

We may also enjoy a pleasant drive in visiting the

OLD SPANISH FORT.

We first go out Canal street, and down the shell road until we reach St. Patrick street, near the cemeteries. Turning to the right, passing the city park, we take the road thrown up along the Orleans Canal, a small drainage outlet, and at the lake cross over to the mouth of Bayou St. John, where is situated this celebrated old fort, one of the first fortifications ever erected in Louisiana. Or we may pass a delightful afternoon by a drive to

CARROLLTON.

Now known as the sixth district of the city of New Orleans. The road is not at this present writing in every good order, but as our energetic Administrator of Improvements, Major E. A. Burke, is turning his attention to our public highways, it will no doubt be all right before these pages reach the eyes of their readers, at all events our livery stable keepers will tell us whether to go there or not. The route is directly up St. Charles street, and probably presents more beauties than any other ride in our city or vicinity, The most elegant residences, carefully kept gardens, with many fine stores churches and other public buildings, line the entire route, making an ever changing panorama which can not fail to please the beholder.

Another very pleasant drive to

CARROLLTON.

is to follow St. Charles street as far as Napoleon Avenue, go through that street to the river and follow the river up. About a half mile above Napoleon Avenue we come to the New City Park, through which we can drive, enjoying the shade of the majestic oaks which line the broad avenues, From the park we may proceed direct to Hickock's or Schroeder's gardens, or turning down Carrollton avenue, enjoy a delightful drive to the shell road at the new canal and return home, either by the Washington Avenue or Canal Street road.

One of the most rural in surroundings, of our drives is that over the old

METAIRE RIDGE ROAD.

We go out Canal Street to the Half Way House. and then instead of going to the right, we pass directly forward between the house and the Metaire Cemetery, down to the bridge. Here we take the road towards the city, which leads us through beautiful scenes to the rear of and above Carrollton. We now come down the river bank to Napoleon Avenue, thence to St. Charles Street and home.

Another much admired ride is that along the

GENTILLY ROAD.

We go out Canal to Claiborne Street, down that street to Esplanade, thence to Gentilly Road and along the road for about three miles, passing the Fair Grounds and Jockey Club. This is really one of the most enjoyable drives near the city.

If we are disposed we may drive

DOWN THE RIVER BANK,

passing immense cotton presses, all in full working order. Below these we come to a thinly settled suburb, one side of the road being lined with fragrant orange groves, and the other guarded by the swift running waters of the Mississippi river. The United States barracks and the Ursuline Convent can both be visited by this route. The student of history will naturally wish to visit the

BATTLE GROUND,

where glorious Old Hickory and his men, achieved the victory which has embalmed their memory in the hearts of their country men, and made the incident familiar to every American schoolboy. Chalmette is about five and three quarter miles below the city, and a very pleasant method of reaching it, is by this drive down the river bank.

Among the many ways of reaching the

FAIR GROUNDS,

is by driving out Canal street to Broad, thence to Esplanade and down the latter street to this delightful resort. Broad is a shell road and is in excellent condition, while Esplanade is one of the most spacious and elegant avenues of our city. Our livery stables are well supplied with stylish horses many of them noted for their speed and endurance, to match which they can also furnish conveyances of every kind, all neat, elegant and comfortable. On all of our drives, in favorable weather gay crowds may be seen, and a trial in this direction will result in much pleasure to those who visit our city.

HUNTING AND FISHING.

The follower of Nick of the Woods, and the disciple of Ik. Walton, will find as many attractions in the near neighborhood of New Orleans, as in any other place in the world. To those who fish with a silver hook, and hunt with green-back bullets, our markets offer a splended field. The best of fish and every variety of game in season will be found in them, and for a reasonable sum, those who like ease more than "Roughing it," can bag enough to crow over for a month. But to those who not only delight in good things to eat but take pleasure in the excitement of the chase, we propose to point out a few places where they may enjoy the "biggest sport" to be found this side of the Rocky Mountains.

The first place on our list is

MILLERS BAYOU.

to reach which we will take the Mobile Railroad and tell the obliging conductor to put us off at Miller's. When we arrive at the station Miller will will come over in a skiff and take us to his ranche, situated on an island which rises out of the marsh on the borders of Lake Catherine. Miller has accommodations for a hundred visitors, and although not as elegant as may be had at the St Charles Hotel, they will be found comfortable. His bunks are clean and well arranged, and he has plenty of mosquito bars and bed coverings. Should we get wet he can supply a very tolerable suit until our own clothes are dry again.

Old Miller is a thorough hunter, knows every foot of ground within twenty miles of his place, and can tell just where the ducks and the geese are most likely to be found. He will furnish a guide to paddle us over to the hunting grounds and point out the best blinds. He has plenty of perogues and decoys, and will set us just where good shots are to be had. The choice hunting ground here is known as the Seven Ponds, and in the season there are literally ducks by the acre to be seen in these small lakes. We went out there one day, late last season, and after a two hours hunt returned with fifty-seven ducks, among which there were canvas-back, mallard and teal. The same day a friend who is a devoted fisherman, in an afternoon's cruise caught sixty odd green trout, weighing from two to three and a half pounds each. The trip out there can be made in a few hours and the entire expense for board, lodging and guide is very small, and we may add for Miller, that he gives "a good square meal" of fish and game well cooked and nicely served.

The next place is

NICK CHENEYVILLE'S,

the best snipe ground in the neighborhood of New Orleans. Nick keeps the Banditt Cave at Chef Menteur. To reach his place we take the Mobile railroad, and a hint to the conductor insures one being landed at the right place. Here the accommodations are very good, comfortable quarters and plenty to eat, and prices very moderate. Nick has perogues and decoys, and will furnish a guide to point out the proper place for snipe or duck hunting. Some very tall stories are told of the loads of game killed in one day's hunt by some of our amateur sportsmen; for them Nick's is a favorite resort. The fishing is also very good at this place, and we could name several gentlemen who delight in the rod and hook, who have tried the lakes of Minnesota and other famed fishing grounds, but prefer Nick's place to any they have visited abroad.

Going in another direction we will take the Great Jackson Route to Bayou La Branche Prairie, and visit the camp of

LOUIS WIRE,

one of the oldest and most experienced hunters in Louisiana. Louis has lately improved his quarters and can now make visitors very comfortable, but he says that if he cannot brag on his accommodations, he can give those who come to see him, all the fun they want in hunting and fishing. At his place the much prized mallard ducks are found in abundance, and no one who is at all handy with a gun, need fear that they will come home with a light cargo. Rabbits, squirrel, snipe, and partridge are also found in the neighborhood, and a days hunt in the rear of the plantations is always sure to be rewarded with a good assortment of these kinds of game.

Or if we want a

DEER HUNT,

we will take the Jackson railroad as far as Pass Manchac, and then striking along the pass, towards the Amite river, with a good dog or two to scare up the game, we are sure to get two or three fine bucks or does, and when night comes on we can find accommodations at the Pass. Here too the fishing is excellent, and if we wish to angle for the finny tribe, we can get a boat and a guide for a trifling expense.

Dr. S. M. Bemiss has kindly furnished us with the following intelesting sketch, pointing out several very

PLEASANT EXCURSIONS,

which vistiors may make :

The lover of the chase or the follower of Izaak Walton, will find opportunities for self gratification around New Orleans, such as the environs of very few large cities afford. Deer and bears may be successfully hunted within from two to four hours travel from the city. Indeed, it is a very common occurrence that deer are killed within three miles of the heart of the city. During their respective seasons, every species of game bird common to this region, and also, squirrels and rabbits, are found in great abundance within convenient access from the city. If the sportsman prefers the pleasures and spoils of capturing the finny prey, he can choose between salt and fresh water fish with almost equal convenience. Lake Pontchartrain abounds with croakers and the delightful sheephead. Two hours run on the Mobile Railroad will enable one to reach the gulf shore, and visit localities where spanish mackerel, red-fish, speckled trout, sheephead, pompano, croakers, and other scaly denizens of deep salt water may be caught to the heart's content.

Very delightful short excursions may be gotten up by writing or telegraphing to any one of the towns on the gulf shore, to engage a suitable vessel to be ready upon the arrival of a given train, to sail to one of the chain of islands forming Mississippi Sound. Cat Island may be reached in four hours from the city; the Chandeliers in eight to twelve hours; Ship Island, Horn Island, or the Petit Bois, in the same length of time. The fishing around these islands never fails to satisfy the expectations of the skillful angler. Pleasure yachts, sloops or small schooners, may be engaged for such excursions at from three to ten dollars a day, according to size and appointments.

For fresh water fishing, the bayous near the city are famous for the numbers and size of the green trout which they afford. All the streams which empty into Lake Maurepas and Lake Pontchartrain abound in trout and perch. Early in the spring of 1872, the writer engaged at lake end a pleasure boat and sailor, at the rate of two dollars and a half per diem, to make a hunting and fishing excursion around Lakes Maurepas and Pontchartrain. We were equipped with a tent and cooking implements, guns, fishing tackle and coffee, sugar, tea, hard-bread, etc. We occupied eleven days in making the circuit of Maurepas and Pontchartrain; we ascended the Tickfaw, Tangipahoa and Tchfuncta rivers. Between the Tickfaw and Amite we killed two deer, and from every stream we visited we caught more fish than we were able to consume. Our sailor, like most of those who man the pleasure boats around New Orleans, was an admirable cook, and few hotels can boast of fare equal to that enjoyed around our camp fires. I look back to this voyage as the most delightful pleasure excursion of my life. To give an idea of trout fishing in the Tangipahoa, I can state, that an amateur, fishing with the fly, caught in one day's sport over one hundred green trout, averaging, as he supposed, two pounds and one half each.

THE FAIR GROUNDS.

The Fair Grounds are distant from the Clay Statue about three and one-fourth miles, and may be reached by the street cars leaving Canal street, or by carriages.

The Grounds comprise an extensive park of 120 acres, containing, among other natural beauties, many of the most magnificent oaks to be found in the South, and elegant velvety swards of well cared for grasses, which at once enchant the eye of the visitor.

The main building is a commodious brick structure, 200x95 feet, two stories high, well ventilated and lighted from numerous large doors, spacious windows, and well arranged skylights. The building cost $70,000.

At a distance of fifty yards, on each side of the main building, stands a wooden one, 206x80 feet, used for agricultural displays, farming implements, competing articles of produce or manufacture, machines, and all mechanical inventions on exhibition during the time of Fairs.

The machinery department is well adapted to the purpose of displaying to the best advantage, the different rival patents in cotton gins, etc., large steam engines furnishing the motive power for their operation during several hours of each day.

The race course is an ellipsis exactly one mile in measurement, and owing to the position of the grounds, is generally in excellent condition. The ellipsis encloses the Club House of the Fair Grounds Association, a platform for dancing and a base ball park.

There is a public stand on the south side of the course, which is conceded to be best for the purpose on the continent. It is three stories high, seats over four thousand persons confortably, has roomy promenades, broad and easy staircases, spacious saloons, and commands an uninterrupted view of the entire course and enclosure, while the view from the lofty cupola embraces all the city and its surroundings: gardens, forests, shipping, the Mississippi, bayous, the lake, church spires, and beautiful suburbian residences, all forming an enchanting southern scene.

In the south-east corner are extensive flower gardens and nurseries, where may be found an immense and rare collection of tropical trees, flowers, plants and shrubs, which cannot be equaled in any other place north of Mexico. These are under the care of that experienced and capable gardner, Mr. Joseph Muller.

Near the gardens is the Floral Hall, a circular structure of sixty feet in diameter, covered with canvass, and containing numerous small fountains.

Here horticulturists bring their competing floral treasures, which are to the lovers of nature, irresistable attractions during the days of the Louisiana State Fairs.

There is a deer park on the east side, which was the especial care of the late Mr. Slocomb, who improved it at his own personal expense. By the death of this worthy, honorable and public spirited gentleman, the Fair Grounds Association lost a moving intellect, and New Orleans a true friend and benefactor, who was ever an open-handed helper in times of need. On the north side there are large and well arranged stables in which over one hundred horses may be accommodated; in all, the Fair Grounds are a credit to the Association that has them in charge, an ornament to the city, and well worthy the attention of the visitor.

The most complete and extensive arrangements have been made for the Southern States' Agricultural and Industrial Exposition, which will be held on these grounds, commencing February 26, 1876, and continuing for ten days. For months past the able and energetic General Superintendant, Samuel Mullen, Esq., has been in correspondence with the leading manufacturers of the North and West, and with many persons in Mexico and South America, and has received such assurances as lead us to believe that the Exposition will be a grand success.

LOUISIANA JOCKEY CLUB PARK.

Adjoining the Fair Grounds is the fine property belonging to this now famous club, which they purchased from Mr. Luling for $60,000. It has a front of 500 feet on Esplanade street, by a depth of 2,500; an area of about 30 acres, situated on the Metaire Ridge, and consequently exempt from overflow. The grounds are planted in choice shrubbery, and well arranged in all respects. The family mansion, which has been converted into a club house, is a handsome three story brick edifice, with a gallery around each story, and is exclusively for the social enjoyment of the members of the club. The rooms are lofty, large and airy; all handsomely furnished, and employed as restaurants, billiard and dining rooms, parlors, library, reading and reception rooms. On the premises are also, a bowling alley, kitchen, etc., and fine stables, with room for a large number of horses.

The gardens contain a rare and extensive collection of plants. In the centre of the park is a lake of pure water surrounding a miniature island.

The club was chartered in May, 1871, for the purpose of establishing a race course, for the promotion of racing, and improving the breed of horses. By agreement with the Fair Grounds Association, the club has the exclusive use of the race course during their spring and fall meetings, for twenty years, for which privilege they erected the public stand, noticed in the account of the Fair Grounds, and which is to revert to the Association without incumbrance, at the expiration of the lease.

For the information of visitors to our city, we copy the following from the "Rules of the Club House," Article 13: "The President, the Vice-Presidents and Board of Directors, by vote, may extend to any distinguished stranger the privilege of the Club House, during his stay in the city.

Any member of the club may invite to the privileges of the Club House, any non-resident, for one day only, to be accompanied at all times by the member."

OUR HOLIDAYS.

We have often heard it remarked by those who devote their entire thoughts and energies to the pursuit of the almighty dollar, "that New Orleans has more holidays than any other city in the Union," and we might add, that they enter into their observance, and seem to enjoy them with more zest than the people of any other place in which we ever lived. If these celebrations have lacked in enthusiasm during the past two years, business has not seemed to gain anything by the fact, that the ardor of the people has been dulled by the stern necessities of life; and even the most matter of fact of our citizens begin to reason, that "all work and no play makes Jack a dull boy," and the coming holidays, which bid fair to be as brilliant as any of the past, will be heartily welcomed by all classes of our citizens. The greatest of our fetes, and the one that has attracted most attention, both at home and abroad, is

MARDI-GRAS,

a French term signifying, "Fat Tuesday," so called because it is followed by Ash Wednesday, ushering in the season of Lent, which is kept very strictly by Catholics and Episcopalians, and is in some degree observed by other denominations. Crowds of maskers fill the streets in the day time, and these are finally marshalled into the procession of His majesty, the King of the Carnival. It would be impossible, in a work of this kind, to give even a faint idea of the numbers and pomp of this display—companies and batalions of troops, knights and gay cavaliers, the Red Men of the forest and the swarthy Turkos, are all represented; gay banners, glittering arms, gorgeous equipages and numerous bands of music, make up a sight which must be witnessed to be appreciated.

"To portray half the characters seen on this day,
Fantastic, grotesque, classic, solemn, or gay,
Would be just such a hopeless and intricate task,
As to tell who the persons are under the masks.

Here are kings, queens and princess in gorgeous attire,
Knights, pages, and Cupids with hearts all a fire;
And birds of the air, and fish of the deep,
Prosperines, Plutos, Robin Hoods, and Bo-Peeps.
Pompous Sambos and Dinahs without stint or limit,
Ugly imps with long tails, which they whisk every minute
Round somebody's limbs, and then laugh in their glee,
As the Fates or the fairies in wonderment flee.
There are Tantalus, Minoture, Cerberus, Charon,
Chinees with long cues, and the Pride of the Harem,
Gods, mortals and angels, monks, nuns and Minervas,
Immediately followed by hosts of infernals.
Boys in petticoats mimicing pert little belles,
Girls in pants, whose bold strutting their sex at once tells,
Dear old Mother Goose with her silly son Jack,
And the Man of the Moon with the sticks on his back,
Evening Stars, and Auroras, Hate, Hope and Hypocrisy,
And a cods head burlesques the fish aristocracy,
Indeed there is nothing the mind can invent
From above or below that they don't represent,
And in groups or processions, one by one or in dozens,
They pass and astonish our dear country cousins,
Who've come in on a visit in crowds not a few,
To see all the shows and the grand Mistick Krewe,
Which of late years has been to the sight of this day,
The crown and the glory of pageants, all gay;
And whether they represent history or chance,
The Vices or Virtues, common facts or romance,
Their tastes and conceptions are faultless and true;
And there's only one drawback—between me and you—
To their festivals, chaste as fire worshipper's flames,
None know, where they come from, and none know their names;
And whither they go we cannot even guess;
But there is a sly rumor 'mong "members of press,"

That they'r not men at all, but wonderful sprites
Who visit us yearly on *Mardi Gras* nights,
To show us how even a masquerade rout,
May be polished by those who know what they'r about.
We do not pretend to dispute with these sages,
As newspaper men have been truthful for ages,
And laid down to people *what should be the law*,
And of course they are posted about Mardi Gras."

At night the far famed Mistick Krewe of Comus give a torch-light procession, illustrating some well chosen subject, making a spectacle which a leading Boston journal pronounced "worth crossing a continent to see." The festivities end with a grand ball by the Krewe, and a State reception and ball by the King, which are attended by brilliant assemblies, and generally last until the gray dawn of day, The next Mardi Gras comes on the 29th February, 1876, and the most elaborate preparations are now being made for its celebration. We append a table showing the dates on which this festival occurs up to the year 1890 :

1876	Feb'y 29	1884	Feb'y 26
1877	Feb'y 13	1885	Feb'y 17
1878	March 5	1886	March 9
1879	Feb'y 25	1887	Feb'y 22
1880	Feb'y 10	1888	Feb'y 14
1881	March 1	1889	March 5
1882	Feb'y 21	1890	Feb'y 18
1883	Feb'y 6		

Thursday, Febuary 24, 1876, being the Thursday previous to Mardi Gras, will be marked by the grand procession of

THE KNIGHTS OF MOMUS,

which was formerly held on the night of the 31st of December, but has been changed to the Thursday before Mardi Gras, to give additional attractions to visitors who come to enjoy that festival. These pageants, like those of the Krewe, take place at night, are brilliantly illuminated, and arranged with consumate skill and taste. Of course, we cannot give the subject of the approaching display, but our readers may rest assured that it will be well worthy of the festal time, and of the fame of Momus and his followers.

TWELFTH NIGHT

is another festival marked by a brilliant procession and no less social re-union, under the auspices of the now celebrated and justly popular Twelfth Night Revelers. It is known in the church as the Epiphany, and its first celebration was during the reign of Pope Julius I, A. D., 337.

The subjects chosen by the Revelers, are always attractive, interesting and amusing, while their balls are always attended by the elite of our city and their visitors. Next to the festivals, graced by these grand masked pageants which have gained a national fame, the most popular of our holidays is the

FOURTH OF MARCH,

the anniversary of our gallant Fire Department. On this day each company turns out, with every man in ranks. their engines burnished until they shine like gold and silver, decorated with ribbons in the most profuse and artistic arrangement, each one vieing with the other, in friendly rivalry, in their efforts to delight the crowds of people who throng the streets to witness their turn out.

We are proud of our Fire Department, and those who have ever witnessed their daring and self-devotion while on duty, or their gallant bearing when on parade, celebrating the Fourth of March, will acknowledge that we have just cause for our pride. The day closes with banquets, balls and other festivities, at which mirth and good fellowship reign supreme. The great American holiday, the

FOURTH OF JULY

coming, as it does, during our summer solstice, is not marked by the uproarousness which characterizes it in some other cities of the Union. Yet it is generally observed, and is a day which thousands of our citizens devote to recreation and amusement. The grand festivals of that worthy organization, the Clerks' Benevolent Association, given on the Fair Grounds, always occur on the Fourth of July, and are attended by immense numbers of our citizens. They are now so much a part of the day's entertainment that any thing which might take place to prevent them, would cause a serious disappointment to thousands of people.

CHRISTMAS

is with us a home day, a day when all the family gather around the home fireside, and enjoy the spirit of love and charity which is so appropriate to the season. It has of late years received new charms for the children of New Orleans, from the matinees given at the Academy of Music, at which that genial gentleman and jovial friend of the young, David Bidwell, Esq., enacts the role of Santa Claus, and gives each little visitor a Christmas present.

NEW YEARS' DAY

is very generally observed by the gentlemen in making calls upon their lady friends, who keep "open house" and receive them with that graceful hospitality for which the ladies of New Orleans are so justly celebrated.

GOOD FRIDAY

is a church holiday and by the laws of our State a *Dies non.* It is very rigidly kept by the Episcopalians and Catholics, and is observed in a greater or less degree by other Christian denominations. The ceremony of visiting the churches, which is very generally participated in by Catholics, forms an interesting feature of the day.

FIRST OF NOVEMBER.

On this day the several cemeteries are visited and the tombs decorated with garlands, evergreens and floral offerings. It is observed by nearly all our people, and the "cities of the dead" are thronged from early morning until night. A beautiful custom which marks the day, is the giving of alms in aid of the different Orphan Asylums, to receive which, delegations from the asylums sit at the different cemetery gates, and attract the attention of visitors by their continuous rapping on their collection plates. Many elegant tombs are to be seen in our burying grounds, and on this day they are especially worthy of a visit. There are other holidays, of recent creation, but they would present few interesting features to the visitor.

COTTON.

This is the most important article entering into the commerce of our city, and for the handling of which New Orleans is acknowledged to be the best market in America.

The first mention of cotton by any European writer is made by Herodotus, about the year 450 B. C. Its manufacture seem even then to have reached great perfection. It is probable that cotton goods were first introduced into Europe as articles of trafic by the expidition of Alexander the Great, in the year 330 B. C., but we have no record of any manufactory of cotton in Europe before the tenth century, and then, only by the Mohammedans in Spain. Its chief mart was Barcelona, in the neighborhood of which the plant is still found growing wild. The quantity of cotton produced in China is enormous; some writers estimate the crop annually, at twelve millions of our bales. Travelers who have penetrated into the interior of Africa, concur in showing that cotton is indigenous to that continent and that it is spun and woven into cloth, which is used by the inhabitants of all classes for raiment. Columbus found cotton in use among the natives of Hispaniola, but only in the most primitive form, while Cortez found the manufacture in a much more advanced state in Mexico. Cotton goods were first manufactured by the Dutch towards the end of the sixteenth century.

It is said that in 1536 the cotton plant was found growing in some of the country bordering on the Mississippi, and in Texas; but the year 1621 is generally conceded to

E. W. RODD & SONS

Wholesale Dealers in all kinds of

Molasses, Syrups and Coffee,

Nos. 14, 15, 16, 17, 18 and 19 Front Street,

Between Customhouse and Bienville, **New Orleans.**

(OPPOSITE THE SUGAR LANDING.)

Having established a wide reputation for our above brands of C. H. (choice), P. R. (prime), F. A. (fair), and C. O. (common), *pure* Louisiana Molasses, we beg to assure our friends of our continued efforts to please them in quality and prices of our goods and the superiority of our packages.

We are prepared as heretofore to fill all orders for Molasses in Barrels, Half Barrels and Kegs of assorted sizes with dispatch, at the very lowest prices, on the day order is received.

J. W. Valentine,

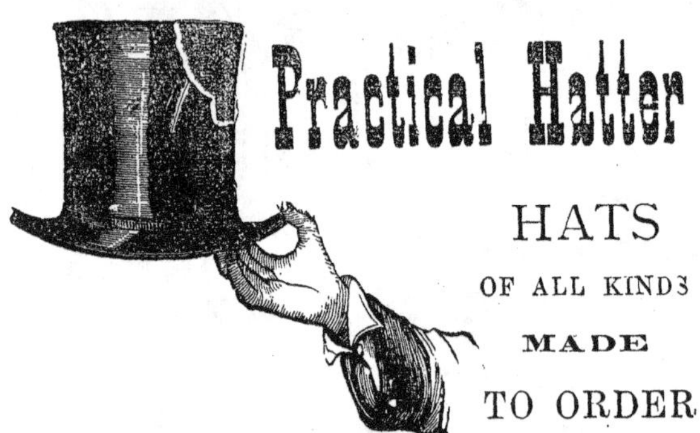

Inventor and Proprietor of the celebrated

POROUS HAT,

State, Country and City rights for Sale.

J. W. VALENTINE,

Cor, Seventh and Magazine Sts.

NEW ORLEANS.

have been the time of the commencement of its culture in the United States. The first mention of the manufacture of cotton cloth in England is in 1641, and of calico printing in 1676.

In this progressive age it sounds strange to hear that the introduction of these factories into that country met with fierce opposition, and that the most stringent prohibitory laws were passed on the subject.

The first regular exportation of cotton from this country was in 1785, and the exports of the first six years aggregated 1,440 bags weighing about 216,150 pounds. To Louisiana belongs the honor of the introduction of the first cotton gin In 1742, M. Dubreuil, an enterprising planter of this State, invented a cotton gin for separating the fibre from the seed, which had previously been done by hand, and was, of course, a very tedious task. The roller gin was introduced a few years later, and in 1793 Eli Whitney invented the saw gin.

The first manufacture of cotton goods in this country was in Philadelphia, in 1775.

The ravages of the cotton worm were first noticed in 1800, and have been a serious draw back to the culture of this plant ever since.

We are indebted to Henry G. Hester, Esq., the able and efficient Secretary of the New Orleans Cotton Exchange, for many courtesies, and valuable assistance in our work.

NEW ORLEANS COTTON EXCHANGE.

It may be safely asserted that this institution has been one of the most successful of its kind in the country.

Inaugurated for the purpose of combining the scattered elements of the cotton trade, so as to be effective in the enforcement of such rules and regulations as were necessary for the protection of all who dealt in the staple, it has, under the wise and able administration of its officers, and with the hearty co-operation of all in favor of justice and fair dealing, placed New Orleans as a cotton market ahead of any city in the Union.

The New Orleans Cotton Exchange was inaugurated in February, 1871, with a roll of 100 members, which, after dwindling down to about 80, increased, under a system of daily news concerning the staple, such as had never before been gotten up in this country, and the development of its wise rules and regulations, to upwards of 300.

The success of this institution is one of the many legitimate results of the rapid advance of the age in steam and telegraphy, which have completely eradicated old ideas and overturned by-gone customs, rendering absolutely necessary a fund of daily information which a few years back was not even dreamed of.

More than $30,000 per annum is expended by the Cotton Exchange in obtaining and arranging information relative to the ramifications of the great staple and its collaterals, gold and exchange, throughout the world.

Daily telegrams are posted on its boards, giving the number of bales received, shipped or sold, and fluctuations in value, embracing every point of moment from Indianola to Mobile on the Gulf, and thence along the Atlantic Ocean to Boston. Its correspondents are at every point in the cotton belt, and the cotton movements of Great Britain, France, the Continent, and even as far east as India are made as familiar to the humblest member as the local movement at New Orleans.

The great principle of co-operation is here forcibly illustrated. Three hundred merchants combine and by payment of $100 apiece, each has the benefit of $30,000 worth of information—so systematized that the slightest change in the great markets of the world either in favor of or against their interests in the staple is flashed to them with lightning speed, scarce a moment intervening between its occurrence and their receipt of the information.

The New Orleans Exchange was the first real cotton exchange inaugurated in this country. Modeled at the outset in some respects after the New York Cotton Exchange, it soon assumed distinctive features, the protection of eighty to one hundred millions of legitimate trade in actual cotton being found of far more substantial benefit than encouraging and fostering gambling in futures, which is almost the sole support of the latter institution.

In lieu of a "future" business, the attention of the trade of New Orleans has been concentrated in efforts to protect the produce of their country constituents from damage by the elements, or spoliation by the hordes of petty thieves that have sprung up wherever cotton has been handled in large quantities since the war.

It is no exaggeration to say that at the lowest calculation forty millions of dollars have been lost to the cotton interests of the South within the past decade from these causes, the evils becoming so engrafted upon the trade as to almost defy correction.

Indeed from the time a bale of cotton left the gin house until it reached the mill to be manufactured into goods, it seemed to be like the public funds, subject to eliminations to supply the "legitimate" perquisites of all through whose hands it might pass—"loss in weight" between the time of original shipment and sale by the factors, notwithstanding the closest watchfulness by the latter, was an every day complaint, and as if this was not enough, the exporter was not infrequently called upon to pay for further shrinkage between the time his purchases from the factor and the period of delivery to his constituents abroad.

How to prevent this had become a problem in the commercial mind. Every system proposed had material objections, but as has been frequently said in great political dilemmas "the cause makes the man," and this was fully exemplified in the matter of protecting cotton, at least so far as this market is concerned. New Orleans is indebted to the large sense and singleness of purpose developed by Mr. John Phelps, for the success of a system of

COTTON SUPERVISION.

that insures to the cotton planter a return for every pound of cotton he may ship to this market. Mr. Phelps has for three successive years been elected to the highly honorable and important position of President of the Cotton Exchange, and has, during this period, displayed executive ability rarely equaled and not excelled by any merchant of this age. Managing a large private business, he has found time to devote himself to the duties he assumed upon accepting the Presidency of the Exchange, and at the expense of strenuous exertions has perfected a system of protection of cotton so thoroughly, that not a balè consigned to a member of the Exchange, reaches this market but what is effectually guarded from the effects of careless handling or theiving, from the moment of its arrival until its final shipment to other ports.

The expense of this supervision last year amounted to about $40,000, paid by receivers at four cents per bale, this sum being made up from the unavoidable loose, such as samples and sample trimmings, formerly allowed to go to waste, or given as perquisites to clerks, etc.

We have not the space to go into the details of the supervision system, and indeed it is unnecessary, as those sufficiently interested in the trade can, we have no doubt, obtain copies of the regulations conveying all the necessary information, by applying directly to the Exchange. Our purpose here is only to point out results. Last season's results of supervision showed a difference compared with the year previous, in the quantity of loose cotton made, of more than 24,000 bales, valued at $1,500;000; in other words: the results of only one year's labors showed a reduction of loose cotton to an amount barely sufficient to handle the staple to proper advantage. As this matter is one of so much importance throughout the entire South, we cannot do better than to quote the following from the sensible and business-like address made by President Phelps at the Annual Meeting of the Exchange, in December, 1874:

" Soon after my election as president, two year since, I called the attention of the Board of Directors to the abuse practised in sampling and inspecting cotton; but nothing was accomplished toward arresting the evil. Last year, upon the election of the new Board, I felt it my duty to again present the subject, and urge that some action be taken. The enormous "city crop," in a season so favorable for handling cotton as was that of last year, convinced me that this evil was still increasing; that it was a serious injury to the cotton trade of this city, and that it demanded prompt and effectual action for its suppression.

You are all familiar with the rules adopted to this end; their working has more than satisfied my expectations, and now that the system of supervision has become general, I think this blot upon the cotton trade of our city has been removed.

It is often said that all such rules and regulations are foreign to the objects sought in the formation of the Exchange; I dissent entirely from this view. The principle of association is one of the most powerful agents of modern times; the great object of our organization is to accomplish ends impossible in our individual capacity.

The charter declares the purpose of establishing the Exchange to be: "To provide suitable rooms; to adjust controversies between members; to establish just and equitable principles, uniform usages, rules and regulations, and standards for classifications, which shall govern all transactions connected with the cotton trade, and to increase the facilities and amount of cotton business in the city of New Orleans."

I am fully convinced that the great evil and abuse in sampling and inspecting cotton could not have been stopped by individual action; and that it only could be done by the power of the Exchange.

I also think many of our members have labored under erroneous views of their rights and duties under the Constitution and By-Laws.

To reap the advantage of an association of this kind, every member must surrender his right of individual action, and be governed by the rules and regulations established by the majority so long as he is a member of the Exchange. It is so in our political organization.

We surrender certain individual rights for the protection afforded by the laws; the only difference is, that in one case he can withdraw; in the other he must yield obedience and has no option."

The views herein expressed have since been practically demonstrated, and the trade of New Orleans is now a unit in upholding the system therein referred to. Other cities are adopting the same provisions, but to the Cotton Exchange and its president will always remain the honor of having successfully inaugurated a system of prevention of fraud and rascallity in the commerce of a great people, which will last so long as New Orleans remains a city.

COTTON PRESSES.

The immense amount of cotton annually received and shipped at our port, gives to the cotton press interest an importance second to none in the city. It is estimated that the cotton press proprietors of our city represent fully seven millions of dollars worth of property. The presses are all well and substantially built, supplied with the latest and most approved machinery, and operated by steam.

The first cotton press ever used in this city was started about the year 1800, by James Freret, father of that universally esteemed citizen, the late James P. Freret. It was located on Royal street, and was worked by hand power.

Mr. John Adems Paxton, in his directory published in 1823, speaks of the extensive fire proof cotton presses of Mr. V. Rillieux, erected in 1806, which were located at the corner of Tchoupitoulas and Poydras street, having fronts on both streets and on Magazine.

To Mr. Rillieux belongs the honor of having put down the first street pavement ever laid in this city, he having, for the convenience of his business paved "with pebble stones" the streets in front of his presses. In former years there was a cotton press on Carondelet street, between Union and Perdido, in the heart of what is now the cotton market, the offices of the principal cotton factors and brokers being in that neighborhood.

The following Tariff of Charges, for the year ending August 31st, 1876, has been adopted by the proprietors of cotton presses here :

COMPRESSING.

For foreign ports, direct or coastwise, whether by steam, sail or railroad, per bale............ 75 c.

For coastwise ports, steam, sail or railroad per bale .... 60 c.

CHARGES TO SHIPPERS.

Drayage to ship and labor, per bale............ 25 c.
Labor on all cottons hauled by shippers, per bale 10 c.
Covering sample holes, covers furnished by press 15 c.
Covering sample holes with shippers' patches.... 5 c.
Extra bands each........................... 12½c.
On cotton ship marked, not ordered the day it is weighed, storage and labor per bale, with the privilege of remaining three days...... 10 c.
After three days, storage for first month, including the three days .... 30 c.

SMALL NUMBERS.

On small numbers the charge for labor and storage for any period from 1st October, 1875, to 31st August, 1876, per bale............. 30 c.
Extra drayage on cotton returned from ship, steamer or railroad, each way 12½c. to be paid by shipper together, per bale........ 25 c.
Labor on same.............................. 10 c.
For forwarding cotton....................... 25 c.

On all cotton ship marked or small numbered, removed from one press to another for the purpose of storage or compression, or shipped without being compressed, per bale 25c. to be paid by the purchaser upon the delivery of the cotton.

Cotton taken by original planter's mark will, if removed upon the day it is received and weighed, be delivered free of charge.

Some of our cotton presses are closed at present. For the benefit of those of our readers who wish to visit those now working, we append the following list:

ATLANTIC PRESS

M. J. Zunts & Co., proprietors. This press and extensive yards is on North Peters street, between Montegut and Cluet. The Levee Street Line, green cars, leaving Canal street opposite the Custom-House, go directly in front of the main yard. The red car, Dauphine Street Line, leaving from front of the Clay Statue, will also carry passengers to Montegut street, within two blocks of the press.

COMMERCIAL PRESS,

Smith & Goldsmith, proprietors. To reach this press visitors will take the Annunciation line, (red cars,) leaving Canal street, opposite Camp. The press occupies the square bounded by Richard, Market, St. Thomas and Chippewa streets.

CRESCENT CITY PRESS.

Sam Boyd & Co., proprietors, This press is situated on the corner of Tchoupitoulas and Race streets. The Tchoupitoulas Street Line, yellow cars, leaving Canal street from the front of the Fountain (opposite Camp street,) will take passengers to this press.

CANAL STREET PRESS.

J. C. Van Wickle, proprietor. This press, one of the best arranged in our city, is on Canal street, between Robertson and Claiborne. The Canal street cars from the front of the Touro Buildings, pass in front of this press.

JACKSON PRESS.

O'Brien & Co., proprietors. Those who wish to visit this press should take the Girod street cars, leaving Canal street near the levee. The press is in the square bounded by Howard, Freret, Perdido and Poydras, and only a short distance from the Gas Works.

KENTUCKY PRESS.

Herndon & Krumbhaar, proprietors. This press with large yards adjoining, is at the corner of Tchoupitoulas and Terpsichore streets. The Tchoupitoulas Street Line, yellow cars, leaving Canal street near the Fountain, pass the press.

LEVEE STEAM PRESS,

J. C. Denis, President, office, No. 57 Carondelet street, was erected in 1832, and is one of the best arranged presses in the country. It is located on North Peters street, between St. Ferdinand and Montegut. The Levee street line (green cars) leaving Canal street, opposite the Custom House, pass this press.

J. W. LEFFINGWELL, M. D.,

Has permanently established his Medical and Surgical Institute and Dispensary at

No. 230 CANAL STREET,

CHRONIC DISEASES MADE A SPECIALTY.

Private diseases cured in a few days. Catarrh, Ulcers of the Nose, Mouth and Throat, Diseases of the Lungs, Heart, Stomach, Bowels, Liver, Kidneys, Bladder, Diabetes, Dropsy, Diseases of Children and Females, Nervous Prostration, Fits, Epilepsy, Chorea, Palsy, Rheumatism, Ague, Scrofula, Varicose Veins, Discoloration, and other Skin Diseases, treated successfully.

Call and see his newly invented instruments and apparatus for the examination and treatment of the cavities of the Nose, Throat, Eye, Ear, and other internal organs.

Patients at a distance treated by mail and express. Send stamp for circular on private diseases and for answer to letters. The poor will be charged only the cost of medicines,

Office hours from 10 a. m. to 4 p. m. and from 6 to 8 p. m. Sundays from 10 a. m. to. 1 p. m.

The following are a few of the remarkable cases cured; each one of whom had received previous treatment by from one to several of the most eminent physicians in the city, and many of whom are well-known, respectable citizens of New Orleans.

DANIEL SCHNEIDER, Residence St. Louis—Chronic Dysentery of eight months duration, much emaciated, discharged cured in two weeks.

MRS. E. CLAPP, Residence Natchez—Abscess of the liver, pain and soreness intense, cured in two months.

MISS KATIE, daughter of Senator Brewster, Monroe, Ouachita, La —Had Ulceration of Nose and Throat, with constant offensive purulent discharge, has been well over a year.

PROFESSOR DEERING, Straight University, La—Bronchitis and Catarrh of throat and nose of eight years duration, cured in two months.

THEODORE GRANT, 307 Melpomene Street—Removed a fibrous tumor from nostril and another from the antrum. A Cavity in the cheek bone of eight years existence, very painful and must have proved fatal in a few weeks. He has now, about a year since the operation, good health and his natural appearance. It is an operation requiring rare skill and one which but few surgeons dare undertake.

CHARLES F. KLEIN, Jefferson Parish—Chronic Ague, Enlargement of the Spleen and Heart, of two years duration.

J. E. BURLAGE, 131 St. Andrew Street—Cured of Heart Disease.

MRS. SAMUEL LEWIS—Two years blind, made to see.

DR. MARTIN BELLERY, Corner Canal and Villere Streets—Was confined to his bed eight months with Sciatic Rheumatism, cured in three months.

LOUISIANA PRESS,

E. K. Bryant, proprietor. This press is situated on St. Thomas, between Terpsichore and Robin streets. Either the Tchoupitoulas (yellow car) or Annunciation (red car) lines will take passengers to the press. The extensive yards belonging to the press are in the immediate neighborhood of it.

NATCHEZ PRESS.

L. A. Levy, Jr., proprietor. This press and its yards, capable of storing thousands of bales of the fleecy staple, is situated on Dauphine street, between Press and Montegut. The Dauphine cars, from Clay Statue, Canal street, convey passengers to the press.

ORLEANS PRESS,

Sam. Boyd & Co., proprietors. This edifice, which is, we believe, the largest of the kind in the world, occupies the square bounded by South Front, South Peters, Thalia and Terpsichore streets. It was built in 1833-35, from designs made by Charles F. Zimpel, and the original cost was over $750,000. The Tchouptioulas street line (yellow car) leaving Canal street, opposite Camp, will convey passengers within one square of the press.

PENN'S PRESS,

Herndon & Krumbhaar, proprietors. This is another very large press, supplied with the most improved machinery. It is located on Tchoupitoulas, corner of Terpsichore street, and the Tchoupitoulas street car passes the press. The Anchor Yard belonging to the same firm is in the near neighborhood.

PLANTERS' PRESS,

Abbott, Randolph & Johnson, proprietors. This press is situated between Richard, Market, Annunciation and Constance streets. The Annunciation line (red car) leaving Canal street, opposite Camp, passes in front of the press.

PELICAN PRESS,

Sam. Boyd & Co., proprietors. Is on Tchoupitoulas, between St. Mary and St. Andrew streets. The Tchoupitoulas street car will carry passengers to the press.

SHIPPERS' PRESS,

Sam. Boyd & Co., proprietors. Those who wish to visit this press should take the Tchoupitoulas street car. The press is on South Front, between Henderson and Robin streets.

UNION PRESS,

A. P. Mason, proprietor. This press is on South Peters, between Terpsichore and Henderson streets. The Tchoupitoulas street cars will take passengers to it.

VIRGINIA PRESS,

Lewis & Lynd, proprietors. Parties wishing to go to this press should take the Tchoupitoulas street cars from Canal, opposite Camp street. The press is on Tchoupitoulas, between Richard and Market streets.

STREET RAILROADS.

New Orleans is very justly celebrated for the excellence of her city railways. They form a network which extends from Canal street, the centre of business and fashion, to the extreme suburbs, affording easy and cheap transportation. The tracks are well laid and the cars and mules are all in good condition. For the information of our readers we append the following description of their routes :

NEW ORLEANS AND CARROLLTON RAILROAD COMPANY.

This road is one of the old land marks of our city, being the second railroad built and put in operation here. The distance to Carrollton, now the Seventh District of our city, is about six miles, and is through one of the most spacious avenues of our city, lined on either side by elegant residences, with well kept gardens to please the eye and gratify the taste. The cars for Carrollton are painted green, and leave the corner of Canal and Baronne streets every five minutes during the day. At Louisiana Avenue and Napoleon Avenue there are branches running to the river, connecting with ferries, and carrying passengers without any additional charge.

Above Napoleon Avenue dummy engines are used, which enables the company to land passengers in Carrollton in a very short time. Once there, a visit to the famous gardens connected with the Hickock's Hotel, or Schroeders, or a walk along the high levee which lines the river bank, or among the orange and bananna groves of this suburban retreat, will well repay the stranger.

The entire cost of the trip to Carrollton and return is but twenty cents, and is one of the most enjoyable excursions that visitors can make.

The Jackson street cars are red, and leave the same place, taking passengers through Baronne, St. Charles and Jackson streets to the river, where there is a ferry which crosses every five minutes. By this line persons can visit Trinity, St. Alphonsus, St. Mary's and Notre Dame Churches, the Jewish Widow's and Orphan's Home, the Protestant Episcopal Home, and that flourishing district of our city, around the Magazine Market, known as the upper city. Gen. G. T. Beauregard is President of this Company, and by his admirable management of its affairs, has added fresh reasons for the respect and esteem in which he is held by his fellow citizens. Mr. P. McBride is the Secretary, and Mr. S. R. Proctor the Superintendant, of the Company, and they discharge their duties with faithful regularity, and are courteous to all who come to them for business or information. The office of the Company is at No. 17 Baronne street.

ORLEANS STREET RAILROAD COMPANY.

Visitors will find the rides over the lines run by this road among the most pleasant to be found here. The cars run through the most interesting portion of the original city, passing houses which have a history dating back to almost the commencement of civilization on this continent.

The Dauphine line, a blue car, leaves the neutral ground on Canal street, in front of the Clay Statue, goes out that street to Dauphine, down to Dumaine street, and thence to Bayou St. John, carrying passengers to the spot where the first landing was effected, now made attractive by the houses of the St. John and Pelican Rowing Clubs; the Magnolia Gardens, and the Shooting Parks of the New Orleans and Crescent City Rifle Clubs. Returning these cars pass the Louisiana Jockey Club House and Fair Grounds. The green car, also leaving the front of Clay Statue, goes the same route as the blue car as far as Broad street, and thence to the station, taking passengers to the Fair Grounds and Louisiana Jockey Club. The Company also has a line of cars going from the French Market out Broad street to the Fair Grounds and Jockey Club Grounds, and back through Ursuline street. This will enable visitors, after seeing the French Market, to go to the Fair Grounds, Louisiana Jockey Club Park and Bayou St. John, and return to Canal street by the blue car run by the same company.

Mr. James Plaisent, the well known importer of wines and liquors, No. 8 St. Louis street, is President of this Company. He is a gentlemen who is fully imbued with the spirit of enterprise which characterizes this age; and on all holiday occasions extra accommodations are offered to passengers, which insures the comfort of all. In fact, the cars of this Company at all times are kept in the best of order, and the pleasure of their patrons is made a leading object.

Mr. H. Hurd is the prompt and obliging Secretary of this Company. The office is at the station on Broad street.

CRESCENT CITY STREET RAILROAD COMPANY.

This company runs two of the most popular lines in our city. Their cars leave the Neutral Ground on Canal street, opposite Camp, at the Fountain. The Tchoupitoulas street car is yellow, and goes up Tchoupitoulas to Joseph street, in the Sixth District, a distance of five miles. It passes many of the largest cotton presses, St. Mary's Market, the Water Works, Grain Elevator and the Louisiana Ice Works, where this article, a necessity as well as luxury in the summer season, is manufactured in large quantities. The car returns down New Levee street, affording a splendid view of the shipping and river front.

The Annunciation street car is red, and goes up Tchoupitoulas and Annunciation streets to Louisiana Avenue, a distance of three miles. It passes St. Mary's Market, St. Simeon's Seminary, Annunciation Square, St. Michael's Church, the three churches of the Redemptorist Fathers, (Catholic,) the Jewish Widows' and Orphans' Home, Episcopal Orphans' Home and Clay Square.

Annunciation street, below Race and above Jackson street, contains many fine residences and well kept gardens, which add much to the pleasure and interest of the ride. This car returns down Chippewa street.

The fare on both lines is only five cents.

The company has recently obtained from the city the right to extend their Tchoupitoulas Street Line from its present terminus to Carrollton, and to substitute Lauren's Fireless Engines for mule power, on week days, from Jackson street, Fourth District, to the upper limit, and on Sundays on the entire route. This addition to the road will increase the length of their lines to about eleven miles. The fare to Carrollton will be six and a quarter cents per passenger, for a time, the expectation being that the spirited direction will, at an early day, if a little aided by the city and State, reduce it to a uniform rate of five cents each for all distances

At present the cars of this company travel nearly a million of miles yearly, and carry over seven millions of people, of whom over half a million it is calculated do no not pay, such as firemen going to and returning from fires, policemen and others. Since the present direction took office in April last, no accident, serious or trivial, has occurred.

Dr. Hugh Kennedy, formerly Mayor of our city, is President of this road. Dr. Kennedy is an old journalist, an able and forcible writer, and in his long connection with the public affairs of our city, has enjoyed, in the highest degree, the confidence and esteem of all worthy citizens. Under his management this road has rapidly improved and is now one of the best conditioned in our city.

Mr. John R. Juden fills the position of Secretary to the entire satisfaction of all who have business with the road. The office of the company is at No. 103 Canal street.

CANAL AND CLAIBORNE STREET RAILROAD COMPANY.

This admirably conducted company have fourteen miles of smooth and well laid track, with three distinct lines, diverging in different directions, passing through the most popular section of our city, and carrying passengers where many objects of interest may be seen. The cars are of an orange color, with the names of the different lines distinctly painted in order to avoid confusion—all starting from the foot of Canal street, near the levee.

The Canal and Claiborne Line passes through the entire length of Canal street, the fashionable center of the city, from its starting point to Claiborne avenue, thence down Claiborne avenue, one of the largest and best shaded avenues in New Orleans, to its station and return by the same route, passing all the important stores on Canal street. The Varieties Theatre, Clay Statue, St. Louis Cemeteries, St. Bernard and Washington Avenue Markets, and connects with the Pontchartrain Railroad, by which a delightful excursion to the lake can be made. In order to accommodate the traveling public the company have lately added to this line quite an attraction in the shape of smoking cars. Visitors to the lake via this route will find the transit quick and quite agreeable.

The CANAL AND COMMON LINE passes also through Canal street to Rampart, and thence on Common to its station, and return through the same streets, offering the same attractions on Canal street, and taking passengers to the Charity Hospital, Hotel Dieu, the New St. Joseph's Church, (one of the largest in the Southern Country,) Varieties Theatre, Claiborne Market, Gas Works, Marine Hospital, City Insane Asylum, and other important points of note.

The GIROD AND POYDRAS LINE passes through Girod, Claiborne, Common, to the station, and return via Poydras to its starting point, taking passengers to the Girod Cemetery, (one of the oldest American cemeteries,) New Basin, Globe Theatre, Charity Hospital, Gas Works, Hotel Dieu, St. Joseph's Church, Marine Hospital, Insane Asylum, Poydras and Claiborne Markets, and through the center of the Western Produce trade to the river.

The cars are well ventilated, clean and comfortable, the live stock all in good condition, and the drivers polite and attentive to passengers.

The affairs of the company are conducted by that well known merchant and public spirited citizen, E. J. Hart, Esq., its president, under whose careful and skillful management its affairs have been thoroughly satisfactory. Mr. Joseph H DeGrange is secretary, and F. Bone, superintendant.

The office of the company is at the corner of Camp and Canal streets.

ST. CHARLES STREET RAILROAD COMPANY.

This company, which has always ranked as one of the best conducted in our city, has three lines, viz: Baronne and Carondelet, (white cars,) Dryades and Rampart, (green cars,) and Clio, Erato, Royal and Bourbon, (red cars,) all run up St. Charles street, passing St. Charles Hotel, Masonic, Exposition and City Halls, Academy of Music and St. Charles Theatres, First Presbyterian—Dr.

Palmer—Church of Messiah Unitarian Church, Jewish Synagogue, Temple of Sinai, Lafayette Square and Tivoli Circle. The white car runs to Eighth via Baronne street, and returns to St. Charles via Carondelet and Canal streets, passing Temple Sinai, The Right Way and Dispersed of Judea, Jewish Synagogues, McGehee Carondelet Street Methodist Church, and Headquarters Metropolitan Police and Police Court. The green cars run to Eighth via Dryades and Baronne streets returning to St. Charles via Rampart and Canal, passing St. John the Baptist—Catholic—German Methodist, Trinity Chapel and Christ—Episcopal Churches, Dryades and Second Street Markets and New Basin Canal.

Strangers will do well to remember that the red car of this company, which passes down Carondelet street—one square back of St. Charles and Bourbon streets, goes directly to the

PONTCHARTRAIN RAILROAD DEPOT,

thus affording a convenient route to that popular resort, Milneburg, at the Old Lake End.

The red cars run to the depot of the New Orleans, St. Louis and Chicago (Jackson) Railroad, via Clio, and return via Erato and Carondelet and Canal, thence down Bourbon and Esplanade to Elysian Fields, at depot of Pontchartrain Railroad, connecting with trains for that popular resort, the Old Lake End, Milneburg, thence via Royal to Canal and St. Charles streets, passing many of the places before mentioned, also the new Opera House, State, District and Criminal Courts, United States Treasury and Mint buildings, Third Presbyterian Church, St. Louis Cathedral and Washington Square. This last route is through the old French settled portion of the city.

The fare by either of these lines is five cents each way.

This company is under the able management of Alden McLellan, Esq., President, whose careful supervision has made it one of the most popular corporations in our city. Mr. Vincent Riviere is the Secretary. The office of the company is at the corner of Eighth and Carondelet streets.

OFFICE OF THE

American Cotton Tie Company

48 Carondelet Street.

NEW ORLEANS, March 1st, 1875.

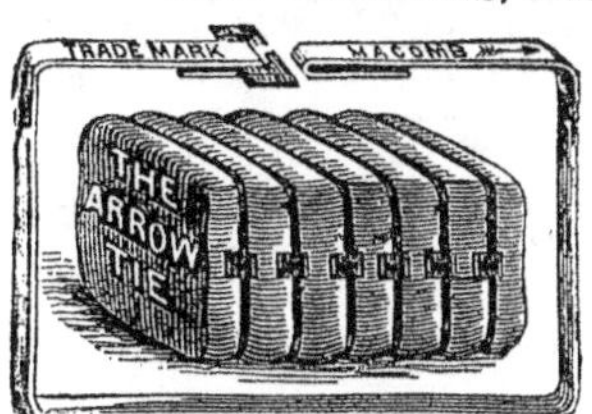

TO DEALERS IN

IRON COTTON TIES,

PLANTERS AND COUNTRY MERCHANTS GENERALY

We are now prepared to meet the demands of all our patrons requiring the well known irrepressible ARROW TIE, and other open "side slot" Cotton Ties.

We have Agencies in the following Southern cities:

New Orleans, La.
Memphis, Tenn.
Louisville, Ky.
St. Louis. Mo
Galveston, Texas,
Charleston, S. C.
Petersburg, Va.
Baltimore, Md,
Mobile, Ala.
Montgomery, Ala.
Atlanta, Ga.
Macon, Ga.
Savannah, Ga
Wilmington, N. C.
Norfolk, Va.
New York.

R. W. RAYNE & CO.

General Agents,

(Late Bartlett & Rayne.)

CANAL STREET, CITY PARK AND LAKE COMPANY.

One of the most interesting localities, in the neighborhood of New Orleans, is the old Spanish fort, situated at the mouth of Bayou St. John, at the point where the gallant Bienville, seeking a suitable location for the capital of the infant colony of Louisiana, turned from the shores of Lake Pontchartrain, and proceeded up the little stream, seeking a place for a night's encampment. The foundation of the old fort remain, and from the ever frowning battlements, on pleasant evenings, groups of gaily dressed ladies, and their attentive escorts, look forth upon the rippling waters of the Lake, while bevies of innocent children, thoughtlessly run about the green, or play with the old cannon, now half embedded in the earth, relics of the days when this was considered an important outpost of the province. Common looking affairs these two cannon are, and in our day, when the art of the destroying demon of war has reached such an advanced stage of perfection, they seem like harmless things, yet they possess an historic interest, and were no doubt considered very formidable affairs by the warlike hidalgos of old Spain.

As the shades of evening steal over the scene, standing amid the ruins, flowers and orange trees, one can in imagination, see that adventurous band, led by Bienville, as they cautiously move their boats up the winding bayou, to plant the Lillies of France on the spot since ever memorable, and found a city on the shores of the great Father of Waters, which in time, should rival in the beauty, virtue and refinement of its women, and the chivalry, fortitude and courtly manners of its men, in the brilliancy, generosity and hospitality of its society, the famed capital of their own loved France.

This place which will always be an object of curious study to those who contemplate the early history of our city and State, is destined also, to be hereafter a favorite resort for those who seek to escape, for a few hours' recreation from the heat, bustle and turmoil of crowded bricks and mortar.

With an enterprise worthy of emulation and commendation, a few of the active spirits of our city organized the Canal Street, City Park and Lake Railroad, to carry passengers to this place, and energetically pushed forward the work, surmounting all difficulties and defying all croakers.

Their cars, drawn by the Remington engines, leave the corner of Canal and Basin streets. The fare is ten cents each way.

NEW ORLEANS FIRE DEPARTMENT

Holds a conspicuous place among the honored institutions of our city. Inaugurated in 1834, it has steadily enlarged its resources, and now stands unrivaled in its sphere of usefulness, practice and experience combining with the jealous enthusiasm of its members to render it the most complete and effective Fire Department extant, and a living monument to the credit of its gentlemanly and efficient officers.

FIREMAN'S CHARITABLE ASSOCIATION.

Office, No. 8, City Hall. I. N. Marks, President ; W. H. Manning, Vice President ; C. C. Flanagan, Secretary ; W. J. Chevallier, Treasurer.

OFFICERS.

Thos. O'Connor, Chief Engineer ; M. Ray, 1st Assistant ; F. Herron, 2nd Assistant ; F. Scheibert, 3rd Assistant ; F. Schneider, 4th Assistant.

The companies are located as follows :

VOLUNTEER, No. 1—Steam.—Hunter street, between St. Peter and Tchoupitoulas.

MILNEBURG, No. 1—Hand.—Pontchartrain Railroad Depot, Milneburg.

MISSISSIPPI, No. 2—Steam.—Magazine, between Lafayette and Girod streets.

AMERICAN HOOK AND LADDER COMPANY, No. 2.—Girod, between St. Charles and Carondelet streets.

VIGILANT, No. 3—Steam.—Esplanade, corner North Galvez street.

HOPE HOOK AND LADDER COMPANY, No. 3.—Corner North Peters and Marigny streets.

PELICAN HOOK AND LADDER COMPANY, No. 4.—No. 77½ North Basin street.

COLUMBIA, No. 5—Steam.—Girod, between St Charles and Carondelet streets.

MECHANICS', No. 6—Steam.—Corner St. Joseph and Commerce streets.

LOUISIANA HOSE COMPANY—Steam.—Corner Perdido and Carondelet streets.

EAGLE, No. 7—Steam.—Dauphine, between Customhouse and Bienville streets.

PHOENIX, No. 8—Steam.—Dacatur, between Marigny and Mandeville streets.

CREOLE, No. 9—Steam.—Esplanade, between Decatur and Frenchman streets.

LOUISIANA, No. 10—Steam.—Dumaine, between North Rampart and St. Claude streets.

IRAD FERRY, No. 12—Steam.—Tchoupitoulas, between Race and Orange streets.

PERSEVERANCE, No. 13 — Steam.—No. 12, Perdido street.

PHILADELPHIA, No. 14—Steam.—Common, between Liberty and Howard streets.

JACKSON, No. 18 — Steam.—Calliope, between St. Charles and Carondelet streets.

WASHINGTON, No. 20—Thalia, between Baronne and Dryades streets.

ORLEANS, No. 21—Steam.—Corner St. Peter and North Claiborne streets.

JEFFERSON, No. 22—Steam.—No. 783, Tchoupitoulas street.

CHALMETTE, No. 23—Steam.—Washington, between Camp and Magazine streets.

CRESCENT, No. 24—Steam.—Dauphine, near Port street.

FIFTH DISTRICT DEPARTMENT.

FIREMAN'S CHARITABLE ASSOCIATION.

Thos. H. Jones, President; E. Quin, Secretary; M. Iver, Chief Engineer; P. V. Nicklaus, P. Whalen, Wm. Sutherland, Assistants.

PELICAN, No. 1—Steam.—Corner Peter and Lavergne streets.

WASHINGTON HOOK AND LADDER, No. 1.—Corner Alix and Verret streets.

BROOKLYN, No. 2—Hand.—Bourney, near Peter street.

MORGAN, No 3—Hand.—Thayre street, near Atlantic Avenue.

SIXTH DISTRICT DEPARTMENT.

FIREMAN'S CHARITABLE ASSOCIATION.

Eugene May, President; John C. Bach, Vice President; Geo. Weiss, Treasurer; C. C. Piper, Secretary.

PIONEER, No. 1—Steam.—Magazine, between Berlin and Milan streets.

HOME HOOK AND LADDER, No. 1.—Marengo near Magazine street.

PROTECTOR, No. 2—Steam.—Corner Pitt street and Napoleon Avenue.

YOUNG AMERICA, No. 3—Hand.—Magazine, near Cadiz street.

SEVENTH DISTRICT DEPARTMENT.

FIREMAN'S CHARITABLE ASSOCIATION.

T. L. Preston, President ; C. W. Besancon, Vice President , Geo. Geier, Secretary ; H. Lorhte, Treasurer ; P. Mitchell, Chief Engineer ; H. Morse, John Pfeiffer, A. Arbo, Assistants.

CARROLLTON, No. 1.—Dublin, between Second and Hampson streets.

STAR HOOK AND LADDER COMPANY, No. 1.—Madison, between Hampson and Second streets.

INDEPENDENT COMPANY, No. 2.—Leonidas, between Burthe and Third streets.

HOOK AND LADDER COMPANY, No. 2.—Adams, between Second and Hampson streets.

FRIENDSHIP COMPANY, No. 3.—Hampson, between Adams and Burdette streets.

THE METROPOLITAN POLICE.

Office of the Superintendant, No. 124 Carondelet street.

COL. W. F. LOAN, Superintendant.

MAJ. P. S. BOYLE, SECRETARY.

The First Precinct is bounded by Canal, Delord, New Canal and Broad streets. Captain Jacob Gray commanding. There are in this precinct, 76 Patrolmen. The station is in Davidson's Court, on Carondelet, near Lafayette street.

The Second Precinct is bounded by Delord, Felicity Road, land boundaries of Harbor Precinct, and Broad street. Captain G. J. Schreiber commanding. There are in this precinct 28 patrolmen. The station is on the corner of Chippewa and Terpsichore streets.

The Third Precinct is bounded by Canal, Esplanade, Rampart streets, and land boundaries of Harbor Precinct. This precinct employs 44 patrolmen. Captain H. T. Lawler commanding. The station is on Chartres street, opposite Jackson Square.

The Fourth Precinct is bounded by Canal, Rampart, Esplanade streets, and rear of city. This precinct is commanded by Captain Peter Josephs, and numbers 33 men. The station is corner of Marais and Orleans streets.

The Fifth Precinct is bounded by Rampart, Esplanade streets, lower limits and rear of the city. Captain Octave Ray commanding. There are 53 patrolmen in this precinct. Station on Elysian Fields, near Greatmen street.

Sixth Precinct is bounded by Felicity Road, river and upper limits of city to Broad street, and commanded by Captain Thos. Flanagan. There are 40 patrolmen in this precinct. Station, corner of Rouseau and Jackson streets.

Seventh Precinct, (Sub-Precinct, late City of Carrollton,) Captain J. W. Wilson in command. Station on Magazine street, near Napoleon Avenue. 26 men in this precinct.

Eighth Precinct, (Algiers,) Sergeant Eugene Rapp commanding. Station in the Court House, 5th district. 12 patrolmen in this precinct.

Ninth Precinct, (Harbor,) commanded by Captain Boyd Robinson. There are 30 men in this precinct. Station corner of Canal street and the levee.

Mounted Precinct, (Suburban Sub-Precinct,) Sergeant P. Taylor commanding. Station on Canal street, opposite the St. Patrick's Cemeteiries. There are 14 mounted patrolmen in this precinct.

This gives us a total of 8 captains and 2 sergeants commanding stations, and 356 patrolmen.

CHURCHES.

There are few cities in the Union that can boast of so great a number of magnificent churches as New Orleans. All denominations of Christians vie with each other in their efforts to make their houses of worship beautiful; stately edifices, worthy of their sacred purposes; while those of the faith of Abraham, show their devotion to the ancient religion of their fathers, in the profuse and chaste ornamentation of its temples.

Settled under the auspices of Catholics, the first church ever erected within the limits of Louisiana was a Catholic church, the old

CATHEDRAL ST. LOUIS.

Fronting on Jackson Square, this ancient, sacred edifice stands a link between the far past and the present time, an object alike of veneration and curiosity. This famous building is the third erected on the same site. The first Cathedral, a wooden and adobe structure, was built sometime between the years 1728, the date of the establishment of New Orleans, and 1723, as in the latter year, the fearful hurricane that swept over the city spreading desolation in its path, destroyed the "Cathedral and many other buildings of great worth and value."

The second edifice was built of brick about 1724 or '25, and was the place where the worshippers gathered till 1788. On Good Friday, March 21st, of that year, the sacred house was again destroyed; this time by fire. As in the former case, the Cathedral fell amid the almost general ruin of the city, for the conflagration which reduced it to ashes, destroyed nearly nine hundred houses, residences and public buildings, almost the entire city of New Orleans.

For many months mass was celebrated in a temporary building erected for the purpose, and, as during this time no steps were taken toward the reconstruction of the church, we infer that the unfortunate circumstances of the fire must have reduced the priests and the majority of the people, to the very verge of extreme poverty.

To Don Andres Almonester, a Spanish noble and colonel of the provincial troops, New Orleans is indebted for the resurrection of their favorite church, as at the personal expense of that gentleman, the present massive structure was erected in 1794, as were also a little later, the two buildings which stand one on either side of the Cathedral, now occupied by the courts, but originally intended for the use of the priests of this Church of St. Louis.

Although of irregular architecture, the exterior of the Cathedral is of majestic appearance, while the interior is at once grand, solemn, rich and artistic in its construction and adornments.

The altars, three in number, the main altar, the altar of Our Lady of Lourdes, and that of St. Francis, of Assiessium, are masterpieces of religious expression in their design, and are, particularly the main altar, en'iched and beautified with the gifts of generations, and that chaste taste in arrangement of color and shade, that has ever distinguished the creoles of this city.. The ceiling is frescoed in the highest artistic style. The centre picture represents the Transfiguration, and around it at either side, and at the, ends are the Evangelists, the Holy Family, and scenes illustrative of different passages in the Apocalypse.

Behind and above the main altar, is a grand semi-historical picture of large dimensions and exquisite coloring, which at once rivets the attention of all who pass the massive doors of this church. It is a most artistic and poetic representation of St. Louis counseling the first Crusaders, and presenting them with "the blessed banner of the cross," every figure and face in which is most beautifully defined and expressive, and speaks highly in praise of the young artist, Bumbracht, who executed it.

In front of the shrine of St. Francis, in a vault beneath the marble pavement, the founder of the church lies

FACTORS' AND TRADERS'

INSURANCE COMPANY,

37 Carondelet Street.

Assets April 30, 1875, $1,486,215 88

This Company issues Policies on

FIRE, RIVER AND MARINE RISKS,

At the lowest tariff rates.

ED. A. PALFREY, President.

MOSES GREENWOOD, Vice Pres.

THOS. F. WALKER, Secretary.

TRUSTEES:

Edward Nalle. R. C. Cammack.

NALLE & CAMMACK,

Cotton Factors and Commission Merchants,

No. 193 Gravier Street,

NEW ORLEANS.

Liberal Cash advances made on consignments of Cotton, Wool, Tobacco and Produce, generally.

L. C. Jurey. M. Gillis.

JUREY & GILLIS,

Cotton Factors and Commission Merchants.

No. 194 Gravier Street,

NEW ORLEANS.

T. L. Airey. A. T. Janin.

T. L. AIREY & CO.,

Cotton Factors and Commission Merchants,

No. 194 Gravier Street, Opposite Cotton Exchange,

NEW ORLEANS.

☞ Special attention given to filling orders.

Louis Bush, of Lafourche. John B. Levert, of Iberville.

BUSH & LEVERT,

COTTON AND SUGAR FACTORS

And General Commission Merchants,

31 Perdido Street,

Lock Box 2047. **NEW ORLEANS.**

C. L. Walmsley. R. M. Walmsley.

C. L. WALMSLEY & CO.,

Cotton Factors and Commission Merchants,

No. 36 Perdido Street,

Up Stairs. NEW ORLEANS.

buried ; a marble slab set on the lovel of the floor, bears the following inscription, in Spanish :

"Here res's the body of Don Andres Almonester Roxas, a native of Mayrena, in the Kingdom af Andalusia, died in the city of New Orleans, on the 26th of April, 1798, at the age of 74 years. Cavalier of the distinguished order of Charles the Third, of Spain, Colonel of the militia of the provincial Spanish Troops; founder and donator of this church and of the St. Charles Hospital; founder of the Hospital of the Larzarines; founder of the Ursuline Convent; founder of the Girl's School, and founder of the Presbatary, all of which he built in this city at his expense. Rest in peace." In front of the altar of Our Lady of Lourdes lie three of the Marigney de Mandeville family, and set in the walls, to the left side of the main altar, are memorial tablets, en which are inscribed the names of some of the Bishops who have ruled over the Dioces of New Orleans, among them that of Archbishop Blanc, the memory of whose good deeds and kind manner are still fresh in the minds of many in the city—indeed, connected with the St. Louis Cathedral are numberless recollections, which, like its beauties, are indescribable. Here, for generations, have chimes been rung for marriages and funerals; hope, joy, woe, victory, defeat, have all had their celebrations within this venerable pile. Before its altars fair brides have knelt on the very spot where their mothers and grandmothers had pledged their vows, and were in time carried to receive the last rites of the church. Here that staunch old hero, General Andrew Jackson, bowed the head and bent the knee amid his veterans, as the *Te Deum* ascended in thanksgiving for the victory of our country over a foreign foe. Here, in our own day, banners have been blessed, which, although they were furled in defeat, were never dishonored by the grasp of a coward, or stained by the disgrace of an avoidable surrender. Here later day heroes assemble in commemoration of dead comrades, whose blood, shed for our liberties, has scarce dried upon our streets. Indeed, the Cathedral seems to be the House of Prayer which all denominations, irrespective of religious prejudice, choose as a place in which to offer public petition or hymn of praise, in all cases where common calamities or successes constrain devotion to the Great Director of human affairs.

The Cathedral is under the direction of the Most Rev. N. J. Perche, Rev. J. Rouxel, first assistant, Rev. H. M. Mignot. Rev. J. B. Laport, and Rev. M. Palmer, assistants.

The hours for servicee are as follows: Week masses, 6, 6½ and 7 o'clock, A. M., Sundays, in summer; 6, 7, 8 and 9 o'clock, A. M., in winter; 6, 7, 8, 8½ and 10, A. M.; Vespers on Sundays, in summer, 6½ P. M., in winter, 5½ P. M.

The Levee and Barracks line of cars, leaving Canal street from front of the Customhouse, pass within one square of the Cathedral.

CHRIST CHURCH.

This pioneer of Protestant churches in New Orleans, is situated on the corner of Canal and Dauphine streets facing on Canal, and is one of the most imposing and elegant structures in the city. It is built of brick, stuccoed and painted to imitate stone, and is of the Gothic style in architecture. Approaching the city from any direction, the high graceful spire of this edifice is among the first to meet the eye.

A brief history of this church may prove interesting to some of our visitors. We regret that space forbids our tracing in detail. its success from its beginnig till the present hour. In January, 1805, the Protestant citizens of New Orleans, feeling the need of a church in which to hold Divine service, met in the house of Madame Fourage with a view of taking preliminary steps to obtain the ministrations of a protestant clergyman, and to secure a suitable site on which to erect a house of worship. A committee was appointed to procure subscriptions, etc.

On the 9th and 16th of the June following, meetings were held, at which the report of the committee above referred to was received. At the meeting of June 16th, an election to decide the denomination of the clergyman was held, and resulted in a majority for the Episcopalians. The ballot was, as follows: Episcopalians, 45 votes; Presbyterian, 7; Methodist, 1. Total, 53 votes. On November 16th of the same year, a meeting was held, at which two wardens and thirteen vestrymen were elected, and a salary of two thousand dollars a year voted to the Rev. Philander Chase, who, at the recommendation of the Right Rev. Bishop Moore, and others, had come to take charge of this germ congregation.

By resolutions passed at a meeting held April 2d, 1806, the Rector was placed under the ecclesiastical government of the Bishop and convention of New York, until a diocese should be organized in the Territory of Louisiana.

Mr. Chase resigned in 1811, and was succeeded by the Rev. J. F. Hull, not then an ordained minister, who officiated till the December of 1832, having taken orders about 1816. When Mr. Hull retired a stipend of twelve hundred dollars per year was settled on him during his life.

This revered and beloved clergyman died in June, 1833.

Rev. Mr. Barlow served as rector for a short time.

During the winter of 1834, Bishop Brownell of Connecticut officiated, as also, during the winters of 1836 and 1837. In January, 1835, a new church was commenced on the north side of Canal street, corner of Bourbon, and a fine building of Ionic form, costing $48,000, was erected, which was consecrated by Bishop Brownell on the 26th of March, 1837. On April 20th, 1838, Rev. Dr. Wheaton assumed the duties of Rector of Christ Church, and officiated tlll May, 1844, when he was succeeded by Rev. Mr. Ramsey, in the summer of the same year. In 1845, Dr. Francis L. Hawkes was tendered the rectorship, which he accepted. entering on his pastoral duty, January 7th, 1845.

The rapid influx of the Americans into the city, and consequent increase of Protestants, compelled the erection of a larger church by the Episcopalians. In May, 1846, the present church, corner of Canal and Dauphine streets, was commenced under the direction of Mr. James Galier, and the noble structure which is such an ornament to our city, soon

"Raised its graceful spire on high."

In December, 1847, James Grimshaw, Esq., presente a beautiful Baptismal Fount to the church, and we are pleased to record, that the venerable gentleman has lived to see the children of the children who were first carried to this fount for baptism.

In 1849, Dr. Hawkes resigned, and arrangements were made with the Rev. Dr. Camp to officiate temporarily.

In 1840, Dr. Neville assumed the rectorship, and served till April, 1852, when he resigned.

In June, 1852 the Rev. Dr. Leacock was invited to the rectorship, which he accepted, took charge in the fall of that year, and still continues his labors in Christ Church.

This venerable and highly esteemed gentlemen is now in his seventy-fifth year, having begun life in the first days of this present century; yet, is still an earnest and zealous worker in the cause to which he, early in life, devoted his energies.

His appearance is venerable and commanding, his manner a touching blending of fatherly kindness and becoming dignity; his style logical, laconic, suggestive and persuasive; his sermons are a most happy combination of the sympathetic and intellectual, and appeal to the head and to the heart; his influence is unbounded in the circle in which he moves; and daily prayers ascend, that when the Rector of Christ's Church will, "by reason of more strength," have attained "four score years," that many days may still be added to his life of usefulness.

Sunday services, 11 A. M. and 7-30 P. M. As Canal street is the city terminus of all the lines of street cars, any one of them moving towards Canal street will land passengers near Christ Church.

FIRST PRESBYTERIAN CHURCH.

This beautiful large Gothic church, situated to the south of Lafayette Square, on Lafayette street, between Camp and St. Charles streets, is one of the most graceful and time honored in our city.

It is a brick edifice 75x90 feet, and 42 feet in ceiling, The tower and steeple from foundation to pinnacle, together measure 219 feet. The body of the church is admirably arranged, and capable of seating 1311 persons. There are also lofty and commodious galleries on a level with the "organ gallery."

The pulpit is slightly raised above the pews on the first floor, and is elegantly designed and finished.

Throughout the entire church great taste and care are shown in all the furnishings, which are rich, but in strict accordance with the grave and impressive worship of the Presbyterian Church.

Attached to the church is a lecture room 75x25 feet, with lofty ceiling and every convenience for the purposes to which the room is dedicated. There is also a school room of the same size as the lecture room, and a library and two session rooms.

The first Presbyterian pastor in this city was the Rev. Sylvester Larned, who died on the 31st of August, 1820, at the early age of 24 years, much and deservedly regretted. The pulpit of the First Presbyterian Church seems to have been the special favorite of eloquence and erudition from its dedication, as the ministers who have in succession had charge of this church have all been wonderfully gifted as public speakers, and men of most liberal education.

The present pastor, Benjamin Morgan Palmer, D. D., L. L. D., took charge in 1856, and is conceded by all to be one of the most eloquent men on the Continent, and one of the most profound scholars in theological and secular lore. His large, wealthy and intelligent congregation regard him with the most enthusiastic devotion.

Sunday services, 11 A. M. and 7:30 P. M.; Sunday school, 9 A. M.; prayer meeting on Wednesday, at 7 P. M.

The Camp and Prytania, or the Magazine street cars, pass within half a square of the church when going up town, and one square when passing down.

ST. PATRICK'S CHURCH.

This old time church, situated on Camp street, between Julia and Girod streets, is a triumph worthy of the genius of Gothic Architecture, whether the dimensions or the splendor of the structure be considered. The style, taken from the famed York Minster Cathedral, is lofty and imposing, and is regarded as the finest effort in Gothic Architecture in the United States. It is built of brick, roughcast, and colored brown, giving the idea of uncut stone—exteriorly the building is impressive and solemn; the tower massive, lofty and majestic is considered one of the most beautiful on the Continent, and being of great height, commands a complete view of the city and suburbs for miles around, from its summit, which is accessable by a spiral stairway in the interior of the tower. In grave and quiet grandeur, the inside of the church is in perfect accord with its outward appearance; the altars and their appointments being rich and elegant, but not showy. Behind the main altar is a very large and speaking picture of the Transfiguration; at the right side of the same altar there is a picture of St. Peter walking on the waves to meet his indulgent Master, who is represented in life size, extending his right hand to the doubting apostle, when, his faith failing, he exclaimed, "Lord save me;" to the left-side is one representing St. Patrick baptizing the Queens of Ireland, in the famed Halls of Tara. In delineating this historic scene the inspirations of the painter were most glowing, and powerfully descriptive, seeming to have imparted the coloring and expression of life to his touch. Every figure is a study, every face a history of the voluntary submission of the haughty Pagan soul to the self-denying, yet ennobling doctrine of Christianity. These pictures, as works of art, have received hundreds of complimentary criticisms from strangers of all lands and religious creeds who have sojourned among us from time to time; but to the children of the "old country," this one picture of the Royal Baptisms is more than a work of art; it is a touching recital of the days when their sea-girt home was emancipated from the power of oppressing heathenism, through the teachings of their patron saint, and recalls whole volumes of the history of their nation in its pristine glory,

> "Ere the emerald gem of the western world
> Was set in the crown of a stranger."

The church is under the direction of the Rev. P. Allen, pastor; Rev. J. Finn and Rev. M. Kennedy, assistants.

Masses on Sunday: 6, 7:30, and 10 A. M. Week-day masses: 6 and 7 A. M. Vespers on Sunday, 4 P. M.

The Magazine, and Camp and Prytania lines of cars pass directly in front of the church in going up town, and within one square in going down.

McGHEE CHURCH,

Methodist Episcopal. The first church belonging to this congregation was situated at the corner of Poydras and Carondelet streets, but fell in the disastrous fire of January, 1851. Almost immediately after its destruction the work of erecting a successor commenced, and soon this beautiful structure was completed. The McGhee church, located on Carondelet street, between Lafayette and Girod streets, a little south of the the old church site, is of the Grecian Doric order, bold and original in design, combining great grandeur of beauty, with simplicity and elegance in arrangement. This is the oldest Methodist congregation in the city, and one of the most refined and influential of all the denominations of Christians. The Rev. J. Mathews is at present the minister.

Sunday services: 11 A. M. and 7 P. M. Sunday school, 9 A. M. Prayer and conference meeting, Thursday evening.

TRINITY CHURCH,

Episcopalian. This edifice, corner Jackson and Coliseum streets, Fourth District, is one of the most graceful buildings in the country, and noted far and wide for the chaste beauty of its adornments, particularly its beautiful chancel and chancel window. The impressions imparted to the beholder on entering this church are those of simple grandeur and beauty of finish, which charm the senses and exalt the imagination. The antique, magnificent chancel window, "Erected for the glory of God, and in memory of Leonidas Polk, D. D., first Bishop of Louisiana, by the Ladies of the Bishop Polk Society," is the only one of the kind on the Continent. The art of producing such work as this window was known in the middle ages, but lost for centuries, and has but quite recently been restored. We have neither the information nor the space to do more than briefly refer to this surpassingly beautiful creation of art and genius.

Two scenes from the passion of our Saviour, and one of His triumphs are represented. The Last Supper, The Crucifixion, and The Ascension. In the first named scene, the Lord is represented, as usual, in the act of breaking and distributing the bread of life to his disciples, "John, the beloved" leaning on his blessed Master, the other apostles sitting or leaning in reverently attentive positions, each face expressing in its own style wonder, love, devotion; the "apostate" only showing fear. The Crucifixion tells the wonderful tale that can only be told in one way. The cross and victim, the soldiers, the three Marys, and the "multitude afar off." The Ascension shows the "Glorified" ascending from "their midst" into heaven, surrounded by angelic forms. These scenes have all been represented times innumerable in paintings, *painted* on glass, and all other ways of representation, and in the midiaeval ages as they are here, in *stained* glass; glass into which the colors have been wrought. This is the art secret of the work, and when we contemplate the wonderful coloring, equaling the finest of the old masters; the clear and correct outline of every figure; the different expressions of love, hate, fear, agony, tenderness, compassion, sympathy, suffering, or glory delineated on the different faces in the pictures, and reflect that it is wrought by combinations made by the hand in *pieces of glass*, a *faint idea* of the artistic excellence and the beauty of this master-peice of art and ingenuity may be arrived at.

As the church is open for many hours each day, and any one permitted to enter, visitors will find no difficulty in seeing this quaint and surprising production of human skill. The Baronne and Jackson street cars pass the church on their way up or down. At the present time there is no regular pastor, the conducting of services being in charge of the curate, Rev. M. Granberry. Sunday services, 11 A. M. and 7:30 P. M. Sunday school, 9 A. M.

ST. ALPHONSUS CHURCH.

Is situated on Constance street, between St. Andrew and Josephine streets, Fourth District, one square from the Jackson and Baronne street cars, and two from the

Annunciation line. It is built in the Renaissance style and is exceedingly spacious and elegant in design; 70x 150 feet, and capable of seating 2,500 persons. The front is very beautiful, having two lofty towers, on which we believe it is intended to raise steeples. The interior of the church is especially rich and elaborate, having three magnificent altars, carved by Mr. Boucher, of Chicago, and costing $8,000. The pulpit and altar rails are also of wood richly carved, and of most exquisite workmanship. There is, behind the main altar, a very elegant picture executed in Rome, representing the patron saint of the church in life size, which judges pronounce a gem of art.

The whole interior of the church is frescoed and gilded in the most elaborate and artistic manner by Canova, a nephew of the celebrated sculptor. The frescoes on the ceiling represent the Holy Family, the Twelve Apostles, the Evangelists, the Mysteries of Religion, the Ascension of our Lord, the Assmption of the Blessed Virgin, and the Coronation of St. Alphonsus in Heaven, all admired as rare masterpieces. A deep toned, beautifully built organ of German manufacture, graces the organ loft; indeed the whole church is complete in all its appointments, and artistic in finish and lovliness, and is justly an object of veneration and pride to its large and devoted congregation.

The building was commenced April 21st, 1855, blessed August 2d, 1857, consecrated April 25th, 1858, and the interior frescoed and finished 1866-67.

The first pastors were the Rev. Father McGrane, who still lives, and the Rev. Father Duffy, who died not quite two years ago, and rests in front of the altar where he officiated for so many years. His memory is loved and cherished in the hearts of thousands, to whom he was, when living, father, counsellor, friend. The present pastors are R R. F F. Ferreol Girardy. Benedict A. Neithart, James Gleeson and Frederick Faivre, all of the C. S S. R.

Divine services Sundays and holidays—5:30, 7, 8 and 9, A. M, in summer, and 6, 7:30, 8:30 and 10 A. M. in winter; vespers, 3 P. M.; baptisms, 4 P. M.; evening services 7 P. M. in winter; 7:15 in summer; week day services, 5:30, 6 and 8 A. M.

ST. MARY'S OF THE ASSUMPTION,

German. This elegant structure in the Renaissance style, 130x75 feet, situated corner of Josephine and Constance streets, nearly opposite St. Alphonsus Church, of which it is an almost equal rival in elegance and finish, was built in 1860. The ceiling, beautifully arched, is considered by many without a rival in America, for simple grandeur and beauty. The altars were imported from Munich, at a cost of $10,000; and a tower in the rear contains four bells, brought from France, which are noted for their sweetness and purity of tone. The statuary of this church is conceded to be among the finest on the Continent.

The pastors are R R. F F. Maximus Leimgruber, Fridolin Luette, John Heidenreich and Joseph Colonel, C. S S. R. Services same hours as in St. Alphonsus Church.

NOTRE DAME DE BON SECOURS,

French. This gem of a chapel is on Jackson street, near Constance, and is also under the care of the Redemptorists. It was built in 1858. Pastor, Rev. Alfred de Ham, assisted by Fathers Faivre and Girardy. Services on Sunday, 7 and 10 A. M., in summer; high mass at 9 A. M., in winter; benediction 5:30 P. M.; week day, mass 7 A. M.

It seems to the old residents of New Orleans but as yesterday, since the places now occupied by the churches, schools and convents of St. Alphonsus parish, was a waste of marshy, unimproved ground, uninviting and unpleasing to the eye, giving no promise of its present beauty or value.

So great is the change effected in less than a quarter of a century, that the mind is almost bewildered at its proportions, and dazzled by its magnificence. To the unswerving efforts, and persevering labors of the Redemptorist priests, the Fourth District is largely indebted for many of its most beautiful and valuable improvements.

CHURCH OF THE IMMACULATE CONCEPTION.

This elegant church, which is situated on the east side of Baronne street, near Canal, and under the direction of the Jesuit Fathers, is one of the most noted in New Orleans, for its beauty of architecture and quaintness of design, and has for years, enjoyed the distinction of having one of the best choirs in the country, always employing first-class artists as organists and singers ; while the reputation of its pastors, for eloquence and learning is national.

The Jackson and Baronne cars pass the church. The pastors in charge are Rev. Fathers A. Jourdan, pastor; J. J. Buffo, D. Hubert, A. Simond, A. Free. H. Bigly, D. McKinney, assistants. Sunday services 5:30, 6, 7, 8 and 10 A. M. Sermon in English at 10 o'clock; week day, 5, 5:30, 6, 7 and 8:30 A. M. Benediction at 6 P. M. and sermon in French at 7 P. M. Sunday.

CANAL STREET PRESBYTERIAN CHURCH.

This church is situated corner of Canal and Derbigny streets, and is a handsome frame building which was completed last spring. It is very neatly finished and will seat between four and five hundred persons. The seats are free. Rev. M. W. Trawick is pastor. Sunday School is held at 9½ A. M., and the services are at 11 A. M. Sundays, with prayer meeting at 7 P. M. on Wednesdays.

COLISEUM PLACE CHURCH,

Baptist. This fine church, situated at the corner of Camp and Terpsichore streets, facing Coliseum Square, is a beautiful edifice, well located, and has a very large, devout and intelligent congregation. The Rev. E. G. Taylor, the pastor, is a man of great eloquence and liberal education, and is held in the highest esteem, by not only the members of his own church, but by all who are brought in contact with him, on either religious or secular matters. Sabbath services 11 A. M. and 7:30 P. M,

Sabbath School 9 A. M. Prayer meeting Wednesday at 7:30 P. M. The Magazine street cars pass in front of the church when going up town, and within one square in coming down.

ST. ANN'S CHURCH.

This church, situated on St. Philip street, between Roman and Prieur streets, is under the direction of the very Rev. Canon H. Tumoine, and is noted for its excellent music. The organist is Miss Theresa Cannon, so well known to our people for her rare musical talent, which she has used so freely in the cause of charity. At the early age of eleven years she was selected for her present position, which she has filled ever since, with honor to herself and satisfaction to all interested. This talented lady gave, by request, her first concert for a charitable purpose, when she was but twelve years old, and so great was its artistic success, that she received the highest praise from the leading musical professors in the city, as well as the unqualified enconiums of the newspaper critics of the day. Sunday services—7, 8 and 10 A. M.; vespers 3:30 P. M. Week days 7 A. M.

CHURCH OF THE MESSIAH.

This church, which is one of the most elegant edifices of the kind in the city, was built, on St. Charles street near Julia, in 1854–5, to replace the one formerly used by the congregation, which was destroyed by fire in 1851, and which was known as Dr Clapp's church. The congregation, for years one of the most influential and extensive in the city, is the only one of the Unitarian denomination in New Orleans. Mr. Horton, the present minister—who has not yet taken charge of the church—comes recommended in the most glowing terms, as a zealous and eloquent preacher, and the congregation look forward with much pleasure to his installment as their pastor. Sabbath services—11 A. M. and 7:30 P. M. Sabbath School 9:30 A. M. The St. Charles street cars pass the church.

ST. JOHN'S CHURCH.

This superb church situated on Dryades street, between Clio and Calliope streets, is built in the Renaissance style, and is of imposing grandeur, and lofty proportions, measuring 172x75 feet. The ceiling, grained and arched, is fifty-five feet in height from the floor, the groins supported by massive and graceful columns. The pews, 186 in number, are made of black walnut with mahogany trimmings. The organ was built in New York, and is of powerful and rich tone.

All of the decorations of the church, are in the beautiful Renaissance style, but are not yet quite completed. The altars are to be of pure white Italian and Irish green and gold marble. All the surroundings of this magnificent church are of simple yet elegant grandeur, and call forth the most exalted and tender emotions of the beholder.

The corner stone was laid in October, 1869, and the church dedicated in January, 1872. Rev. Thos. J. Kenny, pastor, Rev. J. Footte, assistant. Masses—Sunday, 5:30, 7, 8:30 and 10 A. M.; vespers, 4 P. M.; week days 5:30 and 6:45 A. M.

TEMPLE SINAI,

Jewish. This graceful and most imposing structure is situated on Carondelet, between Delord and Calliope streets, and is, without doubt, the most beautiful edifice of the kind in the United States, combining grandeur with simplicity so appropriately that the beholder is at once charmed and edified. The temples of these ancient "chosen people" have always given testimony of their devotion to the faith of their fathers by the liberality and richness of their decorations, and the Temple Sinai shows that they still delight in honoring God by beautifying "His holy places." The interior appointments of the church are a blending of the same characteristics as mark the exterior, simple grandeur, accuracy of proportion and beauty of finish. The forms of worship are those adopted by the "Reformed Jews," to which body this temple belongs. Rev. J. K. Gutheim, rabbi.

DISPERSED OF JUDEA.

This beautiful synagogue, on Carondelet street, between Julia and St. Joseph streets, is the immediate successor of the oldest Jewish house of worship in New Orleans. The first temple, formerly a church edifice, corner of Canal and Bourbon streets, was presented to the congregation by the late Judah Turo, in, we believe, 1847. A few years later, the building needing extensive repairs, it was determined to pull it down and build further up town. In pursuonce of this resolution the present edifice was built.

The mode of service is according to the Shepardic ritual somewhat modernized. Rev. Joseph H. M. Chumaceiro, rabbi.

We give below a list of the other principal churches of all denominations :

BAPTIST CHURCHES.

FIRST AFRICAN CHURCH—224 Howard street.—Rev. Nelson D. Saunders, pastor. Sabbath services 11 A. M., 3 and 7:30 P. M. Sunday, Monday and Thursday, 7:30 P. M.

FIFTH CHURCH—Colored.—Jackson, near Magnolia. Sunday services 11 A. M. and 7:30 P. M. Sunday School 9 A. M. Prayer meetings—Sunday 6 A. M.; Mondays and Thursdays, 7:30 P. M.

FIRST CHURCH —Magazine corner second. Sabbath services, 11 A. M. and 7:30 P. M.; Sunday School, 9 A. M. Prayer meeting, Thursday 7:30; ladies' prayer meeting, 10 A. M. Tuesday.

FIRST FREE MISSION BAPTIST CHURCH—Colored.—Common, between South Claiborne and South Derbigny.

UNION CHURCH — Colored. — Union, between North Prieur and North Johnson.

CATHOLIC CHURCHES.

Diocese of New Orleans—Roman Catholic—280 Chartres street ; Most Rev. Napoleon J. Perche, Archbishop ; Very Rev. Gilbert Raymond, Vicar General ; Rev. Joseph Anstaette, Private Secretary. Archepiscopal Council—

Very Rev. Gilbert Raymond, D. D. V. G.; Rev. A. Jourdan, S. J.; Rev. A. Tumoine, Rev. T. Smith, Rev. C. Moynihan.

ANNUNCIATION CHURCH—Mandeville, corner Marigny. Sunday masses—7, 8, and 9 A. M.; vespers, 4 P. M.; week days, 7 and 8 A. M.

HOLY NAME OF MARY—Veret, between Alex and Eliza. Rev. H. Bellanger, pastor.

HOLY TRINITY CHURCH—German.—St. Ferdinand between Dauphine and Royal. Rev. Leonhard Thevis, pastor. Week days masses, 7 A. M.; Sunday, 7 and 10 A. M.; vespers, 3 P. M.

MOUNT CARMEL CHAPEL—53 Piety street. Rev. Father LeMaestre, pastor.

RESURRECTION OF OUR LORD JESUS CHRIST CHURCH—Esplanade, between North Peters and Decatur. Rev. Horatio Cajone, pastor.

ST. AUGUSTINE'S CHURCH—Bayou Road, corner St. Claude. Rev. John B. Jobert, pastor. Week day mass, 7 o'clock; Sunday, 7, 8 and 10; sermon 10 o'clock; vespers, 4 o'clock.

ST. BARTHOLOMEW'S CHURCH—Algiers. Rev. F. Bellanger, S. M., Rev. F. Gautherin, S. M., Rev. M. Selle.

ST. FRANCIS DE SALES—Second, near St. David. Rev. Nicholas Simon, pastor. Sunday services during summer, 6 and 9 A. M.; vespers, 4 P. M.; during winter, 7 and 9 A. M; vespers, 4 P. M.; Sunday School, 3 P. M., during all seasons.

ST. HENRY BOULIGNY—German—Berlin, between Constance and Magazine. Rev. Bogaertz, pastor. Mass and sermon, 10 o'clock; vespers and benediction 3 o'clock.

ST. JOSEPH'S CHURCH—Gretna. Rev. M. Halbedel, pastor. Sunday mass, 7 and 10 o'clock; sermons in English and German on every alternate Sunday; vespers and benediction, 3:30.

ST. JOSEPH'S—Common, between Howard and Villere. Rev. Thomas Smith, pastor. Mass, week days, 5:30 and 7 o'clock; Sunday mass, 6, 7:30, 8:30 and 10; sermon, 8:30 and 10 o'clock; vespers and benediction, 7 o'clock.

St. Mary's Church—Archbishop's residence—Chartres, between Ursulines and Hospital. Very Rev. G. Raymond, D. D. V. G.; Rev. J. M. Beronnet, Rev. P. Laporte, assistants. Week day mass, 6 o'clock; Sunday, 6, 7 and 10; sermon, 10; vespers 5 o'clock.

St. Maurice's Church—Hancock, corner Royal. Rev. A. Duval, pastor.

St. Michael's Church—East Chippewa, between Orange and Race. Rev. Thos. Heslin, pastor. Sunday services, 7 and 9:30 A. M.; vespers, 4 P. M.; week days, 6:30 A. M.; Thursdays, 8 A. M.

St. Peter and St. Paul's Church—Burgundy, between Marigny and Mandeville. Rev. C. Moynihan, pastor. Week day mass at 6:30 o'clock; Sunday, 7, 8:30 and 10; sermon, 10 o'clock; vespers, 4.

St. Rose De Lima Church—Bayou Road, between North Dolhonde and North Broad. Rev. F. Mittelbron, pastor. Week day mass, 6 o'clock; Sunday, 7:30 and 10; sermon, 10 o'clock; vespers, 4 o'clock.

St. Stephen's Church—Napoleon Avenue, near Camp. Rev. A. Mandine, C. M., pastor. Mass, 6:30, 8 and 10 o'clock; French sermon, 8 o'clock; English sermon, 10 o'clock; vespers, 6 o'clock, followed by instructions and benediction—one Sunday in English, one in French.

St. Teresa's Church—Erato, corner Camp. Rev. P. L. Massardier, pastor. Mass, Sunday, 6, 7:30, 8:30 and 10 o'clock; sermon, 10 o'clock; vespers and benediction 4 P. M.

St. Vincent De Paul—Dauphine, between Montegut and Clouet. Rev. E. Fortier, pastor. Week day mass, 7 o'clock; Sunday, 7 and 10; sermon, 10 o'clock—one Sunday in French and one in English—vespers, 4:30 o'clock.

Mater De La Rosa—Cambronne, corner Third, Seventh District. Rev. A. Bachlmyer, pastor. Masses, Sundays, 7:30 and 10 A. M.; week days, 8 A M.

CONGREGATIONAL CHURCHES,

Algiers Church—colored—Vallette, near Eliza. Sabbath services, 11 A. M. and 7:30 P. M.; Sunday

M. H. APPLEGATE,

PLUMBER

AND DEALER IN

Cooking Ranges and Boilers,

BATH TUBS,

Water Closets, Wash Stands, Kitchen Sinks.

Force and Lifting Pumps

Of all patterns,

SHEET LEAD AND LEAD PIPE,

Brass and Plated Cocks

Of all kinds.

---

141 .... Poydras Street 141

NEW ORLEANS, LA.

school, 3 P. M. Prayer and conference meeting, Thursday evening.

FIRST CHURCH—Prytania, near Calliope. Sabbath services, 11 A. M and 7:30 P. M.; Sunday school, 9:30 A. M. Prayer and conference meeting, Wednesday evening. Industrial school and Mite society, Saturday afternoon, in chapel.

HOWARD CHURCH—colored—Spain, near St. Claude. Sabbath services, 11 A. M. and 7:30 P. M.. Sunday school, 3 P. M. Prayer and conference meeting, Thursday.

MORRIS BROWN CHURCH—colored—407 Villere, Third District. Rev. A S. Ashley, pastor. Sabbath services, 11 A. M. and 7:30 P. M.; Sunday school 3 P. M. Prayer and conference meeting, Thursday evening.

ST. ANDREW STREET CHURCH—colored—St. Andrew, corner Willow. Sabbath services, 11 A. M. and 7:30 P. M,; Snnday school, 3 P. M. Prayer and conference meeting, Thursday evening.

UNIVERSITY CHURCH—Esplanade, corner North Derbigny. Sabbath services, 11 A. M. and 7:30 P. M.; Sunday school, 3 P. M. Prayer and conference meeting, Thursday evening.

EPISCOPAL CHURCHES,

DIOCESE OF LOUISIANA—Office 92 Camp street. Right Rev. J. P. B. Wilmer, D. D., LL. D., bishop ; W. McW. Wright, treasurer ; Rev. Herman C. Duncan, secretary. Standing Committee—Rev. W. F. Adams, president; Rev J. F. Gerault, Rev. Samuel S. Harris, Rev. James Grimshaw, Thomas Sloo, Esq., Henry V. Ogden, Esq., secretary.

ANNUNCIATION CHURCH — Corner Race and Camp Rev. John Percival, rector. Sunday services, 11 A. M and 7:30 P. M.; Sunday school, 9 A.M.

CALVARY CHURCH—Prytania, corner Conrey. Rev. S. Burford, rector. Sunday services, 11 A. M. and 7:30 P. M.; Sunday school, 9 A. M.

EMANUEL CHURCH—Sixth District, north-east corner Soniat and Camp. Rev. Edward Fontaine, rector. Sunday services, 11 A. M,; Sunday school, 9:30 A. M.

Greek Church of the Holy Trinity—Rev. Glegory Yayas, rector. North Dolhonde, between Hospital and Barracks.

Mount Olivet Church—Rev. Charles W. Hilton, rector. Sunday services, 11 A. M. and 7 P. M.; Sunday school, 9 A. M. Peter, corner Olivier, Fifth District.

St. Anna's Church—197 Esplanade. Rev. J. F. Gerault, rector. Sunday services, 11 A. M. and 7:30 P. M; Sunday school, 9 A. M.

St. John's Church—Third, corner Annunciation. Rev. James S. Harrison, rector.

St. Mark's Church—St Charles between Valence and Bordeaux. Rev. H. C. Duncan, rector.

St Paul's Church—Camp, corner Gaiennie. Mr. Upton, curate. Sunday services, 11 A. M. and 7:30 P. M.; Sunday school, 9 A. M. Daily service at 10 A. M.

Trinity Chapel—Dryades, corner Euterpe. Sunday services, 11 A. M. and 7:30 P. M.; Sunday school, 9 A. M.

EVANGELICAL PROTESTANT.

Bethlehem Church—368 Felicity. Rev. H. Kleinhagen, pastor.

Evangelical—Philip, corner Chippewa. Rev. Ludwig G. Heintz, pastor.

First Church—Milan, corner Camp. Rev. Owen Riedy, pastor.

German Protestant—Clio, between St. Charles and Carondelet. Rev. H. J. Perpeet, pastor.

JEWISH SYNAGOGUES.

Chevre Redushe Mikveh Israel Synagogue—Rev. E. Silverstein, rabbi. 165 Dryadas.

Dispersed of Judah—Rev. M. Chunaceiro, rabbi, 218 Carondelet. Services, Fridays, 5 P. M., and Saturdays, 9 A. m.

Gates of Mercy—Rev. J. L. Leucht, rabbi, F. Hollander, president. North Rampart, between Conti, and St. Louis. Sermon, Fridays, 5 P. M., Saturdays, 9 A. M.

Gates of Prayer—Jackson, between Chippewa and

Annunciation. Services, Fridays, 5 P. M., Saturdays, 8 A. M.

TEMPLE SINAI — South side Carondelet, betweeen Delord and Calliope. Rev. J. K. Gutheim, rabbi.

THE RIGHT WAY—Louis Kaiser, president. Carondelet, between Poydras and Lafayette. Services, Fridays, 5 P. M., Saturdays, 8:30 A. M.

LUTHERAN CHURCHES.

ST. JOHN'S CHURCH—Customhouse, cor. North Prieur. Rev. C. Frank, pastor. Sabbath services, 10 A. M. and 3 P. M.

ST. PAUL'S CHURCH—Port, corner Burgundy. Rev. Christian Moedinger, pastor. Sabbath services, 10 A. M. and 7 P. M.

ZION CHURCH—Rev. M. Turmenstein, pastor, east side St. Charles, corner St. Andrew.

METHODIST EPISCOPAL CHURCHES.

AMES CHAPEL—St Charles corner Calliope. Rev. James Morrow, pastor. Sabbath services, 11 A. M. and 7 P. M. Sunday school, 9 A. M. and 3 P. M. Prayer meetings, Thursday evenings.

FIRST GERMAN CHURCH—South Franklin, corner St. Andrew. Rev. L. Allinger, pastor.

FIRST STREET CHURCH—colored—Winans' Chapel—Dryades, north-east corner First. Sabbath services, 11 A. M. and 7 P. M. Sunday school, 9 A. M. Prayer meeting, Thursday evening.

GERMAN CHURCH—colored — Felicity Road, between Dryades and Rampart. Sabbath services, 11 A, M. and 7 P. M, Sunday school, 9 A. M. Prayer meeting, Thursday evening.

MOUNT OLIVET CHURCH—Rev. William Orange, pastor. Marengo, between Constance and Magazine.

PORT STREET CHURCH—colored—Green's Chapel—93 Washington. Sabbath services, 11 A. M. and 7 P. M.; Sunday school 9 A. M.; prayer meeting Thursday evening.

SIXTH STREET AFRICAN CHURCH—Sixth, between Annunciation and Laurel. Sabbath services, 11 A. M. and 7 P. M.; Sunday school, 9 A. M.; prayer meeting, Thursday evening.

St. Paul's Church—colored—132 Liberty, First District.

St Marys Street Church—colored—Chippewa, cor. St. Mary. Sabbath services, 11 A. M. and 7 P. M.; Sunday school, 9 A. M.; prayer meeting, Thursday evening.

Union Chapel—Rev. George Dardis, pastor. Bienville between Villere and Marais.

Wyndham Chapel—First, corner Dryades. Rev. J. Gould, pastor.

METHODIST, EPISCOPAL—SOUTH.

Algiers Church—Algiers. Rev. L. A. Reed, pastor. Sabbath services, 11 A. M. and 7 P. M.; Sunday school, 9 A. M.; conference and prayer meeting, Wednesday evening.

Cadiz Street Church—Cadiz, corner Coliseum. Rev. James A. Ivy, pastor. Sabbath services, 11 A. M. and 7:30 P. M.; Sunday school, 9 A. M.; Rev. J. D. Parker, superintendent.

Dryades Street Church—Dryades, corner Felicity road. Rev John A. G. Rabe, pastor. Sabbath services, 11 A. M. and 7:30 P. M.; Sunday school 9 A. M.; J. H. Keller, superintendent; prayer meeting, Tuesday evening; preaching, Thursday evening.

Felicity Church—Felicity road, near Chestnut. Rev. John Mathews, pastor. Sabbath services, 11 A. M. and 7:30 P. M.; Sunday school, 9 A. M.; W. H. Foster, superintendent; prayer and conference meeting, Thursday evening.

German Church—Dryades, between Euterpe and Felicity. Rev. J. B. A. Ahrens, pastor. Sabbath services, 11 A. M. and 7:30 P. M.; Sundy school, 9 A. M.; prayer and conference meeting, Monday evening; preaching, Thursday evening.

Little Bethel Methodist Church—Rev. Henry Jordan, pastor. Camp, between Thalia and Erato.

Louisiana Avenue Church—Louisiana Avenue, corner Magazine. Rev. James S. White, pastor. Sabbath services, 11 A. M. and 7 P. M.; Sunday school, 9 A. M.

MOREAU STREET CHURCH—Chartres, late Moreau, cor. Lafayette. Rev. J. D. Adams, pastor. Sabbath services, 11 A. M. and 7 P. M.; Sunday school, 9 A. M., R. L. Robertson, superintendent; prayer and conference meeting, Friday evening.

SORAPARU CHURCH—Soraparu, between Chippewa and Annunciation. Sabbath services, 11 A. M. and 7:30 P. M.; Sunday school, 9 A. M.

PRESBYTERIAN CHURCHES.

AFRICAN CHURCH—465 Villere; Third District.

FIRST GERMAN PRESBYTERIAN CHURCH—First, near Laurel. Rev. John Hollander, pastor. Sunday services, 11 A. M. and 7:30 P. M.; Sunday school, 9:30 A. M.

FOURTH PRESBYTERIAN CHURCH—Liberty, corner Gasquet. Sunday services, 11 A. M. and 7:30 P. M.; Sunday school, 9:30 A. M.; prayer meeting, Thursday evening.

LAFAYETTE PRESBYTERIAN CHURCH—Magazine, bet. Phillip and Jackson. Rev. T. R. Markham, pastor. Sunday services, 11 A. M.; Sunday school 9 A. M.; prayer meeting, Wednesday evening. Pastor resides 179 Constance.

NAPOLEON AVENUE PRESBYTERIAN CHURCH—Napoleon Avenue, near Camp street. Rev. B. Wayne, pastor.

PRYTANIA STREET PRESBYTERIAN CHURCH—Prytania, corner Josephine. Rev R. Q. Mallard, pastor. Sunday services, 11 A. M. and 7 P. M.; Sunday school, 9:15 A. M.; prayer meeting, Friday 7 P. M. Pastor's residence, 152 Coliseum,

SECOND PRESBYTERIAN CHURCH—St. Bernard, corner North Claiborne. Rev. Otto T. Koeller, pastor.

FRANKLIN STREET CHURCH—Euterpe, corner Franklin. Rev. Wm. Flynn, pastor. Sunday services, 11 A. M. and 7:30 P. M.; Sunday school, 9 A. M; prayer meeting, Wednesday 7:30 P. M.; seats free. Pastor's residence, 298 Franklin.

THIRD PRESBYTERIAN CHURCH—Washington square. Rev. H. M. Smith, pastor. Sunday services, 11 A. M. and 7 P. M.; Sunday school, 9 A M.; prayer meeting, Thursday 7 P. M. Pastor resides 533 Chartres.

SWEDENBORGIAN.

New Jerusalem Church—Melpomene, corner Camp.

NEWSPAPERS.

New Orleans has at present a larger number of newspapers and periodicals than at any former time within our memory. For the information of our readers at a distance, we here append a list of these journals, which we can cordially recommend to both readers and advertisers :

Bulletin—Every morning except Monday—A large eight-page paper, Democratic in politics, and very ably conducted. Page M. Baker is editor and proprietor. Although young, this journal being in the hands of experienced and popular writers, enjoys to a very large degree the confidence and esteem of our people.

Bee—Every morning except Monday, and weekly, Saturdays—Dufour & Limet, editors and publishers, was established in 1827, and is the oldest paper in the State ; is conducted with a consistent adherence to principles which commands the esteem of all classes. It is Democratic in politics, and being published in French, it is very naturally the accepted organ of the French and Creole classes of the population. It has four pages 29x43.

Budget—Weekly, Saturdays—Is a handsomely printed family paper, containing a variety of choice reading, which makes it very popular in the home circle. James H. Hummel is editor and proprietor.

Christian Advocate—Weekly, Thursday—The organ of the Methodist Episcopal Church, South. Established in 1851. Robert J. Harp, publisher.

Delta—Weekly, Sundays—Was started, we believe, as the organ of the Democratic party, but independent of politics, it is a very acceptable family paper and enjoys a large circulation. Edwin L. Jewell is editor and proprietor.

DAILY DIRECTORY AND STRANGERS' GUIDE—Was recently established by that experienced, practical printer, John Polk Hopkins. It is circulated free and has secured to a large degree the patronage of our business community.

FAMILIEN FREUND—Bi-weekly, German. Published at $1 a year, by J. B. A. Ahrens.

GERMAN GAZETTE—DEUTSCHE ZEITUNG—Every day except Monday, and weekly Thursdays—This ably conducted German paper was established in 1847, and is very popular with the large and influential class of our people who speak that language. Jacob Hassinger is editor and proprietor.

KINDERFREUND—Monthly. German—Published by J. B. A. Ahrens. Subscription 25 cents.

LE QUARTORZE SEPTEMBRE—Weekly, Sunday—A new paper published in French by Albert Fabre, an old and experienced journalist, a thorough scholar, forcible and pleasing writer.

LOUISIANIAN—Weekly, Saturdays—Republican in politics, P. B. S. Pinchback, editor and proprietor. Is the organ of the colored Republicans of the city.

MORNING STAR AND CATHOLIC MESSENGER—Weekly, Sundays—The only English Catholic journal in the city. Contains the latest foreign and domestic religious and secular news. Is highly esteemed as a family newspaper, and enjoys a wide circulation both in our own and neighboring States. Thomas G. Rapier is business manager.

MEDICAL AND SURGICAL JOURNAL—Bi-monthly—A magazine of two hundred pages. It is under the editorial management of Dr. S. M. Bemis, one of the most skillful physicians of our city. The magazine presents a neat typographical appearance, and contains scientific and literary articles of the highest order of merit. Subscription $5. Seymour & Stevens are the publishers.

NEW ORLEANS SEMI-ANNUAL TRADE GUIDE—D. Webster, proprietor. A handsomely gotten up pamphlet; issued in January and July.

ORLEANIAN—Weekly, Sundays—Wharton & Dawson,

proprietors. A literary, society and family journal; the official organ of the Property Holders' Union. Major E. C. Wharton, the editor, is an old and valued member of the New Orleans press, and is esteemed one of the most pleasing and graceful of writers.

OUR HOME JOURNAL—Weekly, Saturdays—James H. Hummel, proprietor. Is an elegantly illustrated and ably edited journal devoted to the agricultural interests of the South, and containing besides a large amount of valuable general reading, making it an esteemed visitor in every family.

PRICE CURRENT—Semi-weekly, Wednesdays and Saturdays—Louis J. Bright & Co, editors and proprietors. This journal is devoted to the commercial interests of New Orleans, and on all questions relating to its special department, is acknowledged throughout the country as a thoroughly reliable and competent authority. It was established in 1822, and its present proprietors will maintain the high repute of their paper. The typographical appearance of the paper is as creditable as its contents, and the *tout ensemble* presented is justly popular with a wide circle of patrons.

PROPAGATEUR CATHOLIQUE—Weekly. Saturdays—Is a large and ably conducted journal in French, devoted to the interests of the Catholic faith. A. Lutton is editor and publisher.

PICAYUNE—Every morning, and weekly, Saturdays—Established in 1836. A. M. Holbrook, editor and proprietor. Conservative in politics, employs a corps of talented writers and is a favorite family paper, having a wide circulation in the country adjacent to New Orleans.

REPUBLICAN—Every morning except Monday, and weekly, Saturdays—Official journal of the city and State. The most influential and ably conducted Republican journal in the South. T. G. Tracy, business manager.

SOUTHWESTERN GRANGER—Weekly, Saturdays—W. L. Murray, publisher, Sam. D. Elliott, business manager. Is devoted to the Grange interests. A large, well printed and interesting family paper.

S. HERNSHEIM & BRO

Importers and wholesale dealers in

Leaf AND Manufactured Tobacco,

We have on hand a large and varied assortment of Manufactured Tobacco, which we offer to the trade at the lowest market price. We are proprietors of the celebrated Black Horse Leaf Tobacco for the Mexican and West India market. We beg to call the attention of

CIGAR MANUFACTURERS

To our extensive stock of

HAVANA AND PENNSYLVANIA LEAF TOBACCO.

In imported Cigars we have

LA TRINIDAD, LA IGUALDAD, LA ESCEPCION, GOLDEN EAGLE.

DOMESTIC CIGARS OF ALL KINDS.

S. HERNSHEIM & BRO., - - 69, 71, 73, Gravier Street.

J. H. HINRICHS,

Manufacturer of

SHOW CASES,

WHITE METAL SASH,

WINDOWS, FOR SHOW

63 CHARTRES STREET,
Near Bienville,
NEW ORLEANS, LA.

Orders by mail promptly attended to.

SOUTHERN TEMPERANCE ORGAN—Weekly, Saturdays—Published in the interests of the cause of temperance. M. Jones Scott, publisher.

SOUTHWESTERN PRESBYTERIAN—Weekly, Thursdays—Established in 1869. Subscription $2 50. Rev. Henry M. Smith, Editor.

SOUTHWESTERN ADVOCATE—Bi-weekly—Established in 1865. Subscription $1. Rev. J. C. Hartzell, editor.

TIMES—Every morning, and weekly, Saturdays—Stoutemyer & Judson, proprietors. A live progressive and ably conducted newspaper, conservative in politics, and discussing with ability all leading topics of the day Its wide circulation, popularity and influence, may very justly be a matter of pride to all connected with it.

RAILROADS.

The railroad lines now in operation, the New Orleans, St. Louis and Chicago, popularly known as the Jackson Route, the Mobile, Morgan's Louisiana and Texas, and the New Orleans and Texas, are all familiar to the public. Among the projected roads, those mentioned below are, we think, the most important:

NEW ORLEANS PACIFIC RAILWAY.

The problem of a railroad to Texas and thence to the Pacific, has been before the New Orleans public for a time beyond which the memory of this writer does not extend. Several companies have been formed, some of them have built portions of a road and then snspended operations.

Early last spring some of the merchants of New Orleans took the matter in hand, and, we think that we may safely congratulate our citizens upon the fact that, the long hoped for railroad connection is now an assured event of the near future.

The following are the names of the Board of Directors as now constituted; E. B. Wheelock, Hugh Kennedy, S. H. Kennedy, E. L. Ranlett, Alf. Moulton, Cyrus Bussey, Geo. Jonas, James A. Girdner, Emory Clapp, John H. Kennard, Louis Schneider, W. B. Schmidt, Julius Weis, David Wallace, Ad. Schreiber.

OFFICERS;—E. B. Wheelock, President; Dr. Hugh Kennedy, Vice President; E. L. Ranlett Secretary; Kennard, Howe, & Prentiss, Attorneys.

An array of energy, ability and integrity which could not but command the confidence of all classes of our citizens.

After mature deliberation it was determined to build a road from Alexandria in this State, to Marshall, Texas, The wisdom of this course will be readily admitted by every thinking mind, when the reasons are stated.

Red River, on which Alexandria is situated, is navigable for light boats all the year, and for nine months for large size boats. Thus when this road is completed New Orleans will be brought into direct communication with the richest and most fertile sections of Northern Louisiana and Western Texas. But, say the croakers, a railroad ending at Alexandria is not a New Orleans road! In answer to this, the gentlemen of the New Orleans, Pacific Railroad Company, point to the fact that two roads, Morgan's Louisiana and Texas, and the New Orleans and Texas, are already completed more than half the distance to Alexandria, making it certain tnat when their line from Marshall to Alexandria is in running order, one or both of these corporations will push forward their enterprise, so as to reap the rich harvest which the freights and passengers of the new road will be sure to yield.

The New Orleans Pacific Railway is therefore no visionary enterprise, it is governed by energy, wisdom and prudence, and in the immense advantages which it will bring to our city, the names of the public spirited and self-sacrificing citizens who have given their time and talents to the undertaking must not be forgotten.

NEW ORLEANS AND NORTHEASTERN RAILROAD.

One of the most important railroad lines ever projected for our city, is that named in the heading of this article. A convenient, cheap and expeditious route to a suburban location, pleasant and healthful, is a desideratum long sought by our citizens, and this boon will be furnished by this road when finished.

From the heart of New Orleans, to a place which is ninety feet above the ordinary level of Lake Pontchartrain, where health can be enjoyed, life prolonged, and all the luxuries procured, is only thirty miles.

The line will cross Lake Pontchartrain by a bridge, or series of bridges, the average depth of the Lake at the point built over being only fifteen and a half feet, and the greatest depth but little over nineteen feet. The most competent engineers of America have pronounced this route perfectly feasible and safe, and that it will be adopted is only a question of time.

Reaching the opposite Lake Coast, we at once enter upon a country which gradually elevates as we proceed. The first point of interest is the town of Covington, on the Bogue Talia River, a delightful locatian, in a high and rolling country, which abounds in splendid scenery, and enjoys a climate as healthy and enjoyable as any in the world. The winters are like Indian summers. Spring opens early in February with blossoms on the peach and quince trees ; the heat of summer is moderate, and the unfailing breezes of the evening are invigorating and enjoyable. Within two miles, mineral springs, equal in healing properties to the most famous waters known to the world, will be found, of which the Abita and Ingram's Sulphur Springs, are already famous.

We cannot dwell upon the great inducements held out by this road ; the cheap homesteads, salubrious climate, and beautiful location for family residences, abounding on every hand, but we hope that they may early be realized, and then we are sure that the New Orleans and Northeastern Railroad will soon become one of the most popular of Southern routes.

POPULATION OF THE 17 WARDS

(Carrollton included,) of New Orleans or Orleans Parish, according to the United States Census, 1870, and State Census, 1875.

	U. S. Census.	State Census
Total Population	197,913	203,439
White "	144,076	145,721
Colored "	53,798	57,647
Indian and Chinese Population	39	71
Native Born population, i. e., born in the U. S.	148,461	159,727
Foreign Born Population	49,452	43,712
Male Population	* 93,527	96,682
Female "	* 104,386	106,757
Foreign Born, males, over 21 yrs.	23,106	20,250
" over 21 years., not naturalized	....	5,266
Foreign Born, naturalized	....	14,984
No. Children, 6–21 yrs. of age	* 63,500	58,683
No. Colleges, Universities and Schools	....	168
No. Pupils therein	....	32,433
No. White Pop., over 6 years age, who "cannot read and write."	....	35,318
No. Colored, over 6 years age, who "cannot read and write."	....	37,708
No. Births in 1870 and in 1874	† 6,000	5,350
No. of Pop. over 18 years who have had yellow fever	....	25,071
Total No. of Pop. over 18 yrs. old	* 115,915	
No. of Pop. temporarily absent	....	2,808

NOTES—*These numbers are obtained by adding to the actual figures given by the U. S. Census for the 15 wards of New Orleans, of 1870, *estimates* for the 16th and 17th wards, i. e., Carrollton. These estimates are somewhat too large since they are based on a population of 6,549 assigned Carrollton by U. S. Census, 1870. The whole of said Carrollton was not annexed to New Orleans—only so much thereof as, by State Census of 1875, numbered 5,400 total population.

† The births, estimated from data in the U. S. Census and in the Reports of the Board of Health, amount annually to *certainly not less* than 6000, and to not more than 6,500.

POLITICAL STATISTICS OF NEW ORLEANS OR ORLEANS PARISH.

NUMBER OF VOTERS.	Total of Native and Foreign Males over 21 Y'rs.	NATIVE BORN.			FOREIGN BORN.		
		Total.	White.	Colored.	Total.	White.	Col'rd.
Males 21 years and over in 1870 in the total 15 wards, (Carrollton excluded) by United States census..................	47,712	52,069	12,884	12,185	22,643	22,426	217
Male citizens in 1870 in the 15 wards, (Carrollton excluded) by U. S. census....................................	38,586	....	....	....	....	....	......
Registered voters in 1870 in the 15 wards (Carrollton included)............	36,057	26,861	....	....	9,196	....	......
Males 21 years and over in 1874 in the 17 wards (Carrollton included) by U. S. census.....................................	49,539	26,433	13,322	13,111	23,106	22,876	?230
Registered voters in 1874 in the 17 wards (Carrolltone xcluded)..........	*46,199	32,831	....	....	13,368	....	......
No. of persons entitled to vote, according to the State census of 1875.......	44,392						
No. of foreign born, naturalized. according to the State census of 1875...	14,984						
No. of foreign born, not naturalized, according to the State census of 1875...	5,266						

NOTE.—*Of the 46,199 voters registered in 1874, 28,054 were white and 18.145 colored, out of a total colored male population over 21 years of 13,341, by U. S. census of 1870.

NUMBER OF VOTERS WHO VOTED.

	Total Vote.	Republican.	Opposition.
Vote of 1870	30,400	18.354	12,046
Vote of 1872, as cast, Forman-Mitchell Board	35,807	13,697	22,110
Vote of 1872, as counted, Lynch - Bovee - Hawkins Board	34,580	14,043	20,537
Vote of 1874, as cast, Supervisors of Election	39,022	13,281	25,741
Vote of 1874, as counted by the Returning Board	40,266	14,062	26,204

We are indebted to Prof. S. E. Chaillé, M. D., for the foregoing carefully prepared, valuable and interesting tables.

METEOROLOGICAL MEMORANDA.

Record of Temperature in New Orleans, for the Three Years Commencing July 1st, 1872, and Ending June 30th, 1875:

Year.	JANUARY.					FEBRUARY.					MARCH.				
	Highest.	Lowest.	Average Maxima.	Average Minima.	Mean Value.	Highest.	Lowest.	Average Maxima.	Average Minima.	Mean Value.	Highest.	Lowest.	Average Maxima.	Average Minima.	Mean Value.
1872															
1873	71.0	25.0	56.26	43.50	49.88	81.0	43.0	67.91	52.32	60.12	81.5	38.0	69.46	53.29	61.37
1874	77.0	32.0	63.76	49.67	56.72	77.5	41.5	65 84	53 34	59.59	84.0	50 0	74.79	60.82	67.81
1875	77.5	29.0	59·64	48.15	53.89	80.0	31.0	62.46	48.00	55.23	81.0	36.5	71.22	56.98	64.10
M'n.			59.89	47.11	53.49			65 40	51.22	58.31			71.82	57.03	64.43

Year.	APRIL.					MAY.					JUNE.				
1872															
1873	86.0	45.5	75.98	59.92	67.95	88.5	57.0	82.33	68.03	75.19	92.0	72.0	88.35	74.97	81.66
1874	82.0	46.0	73.40	59.05	66.22	92.5	57.0	85.10	68.72	76.91	94.0	72.0	89.88	75.35	82.62
1875	82.0	47.0	73.51	58.13	65.82	90.0	62.0	85.19	69.64	77.42	94.5	67.0	87.95	73.83	80.89
M'n.			74.29	59.03	66.66			84.21	68.80	76.51			88.73	74.72	81.72

METEOROLOGICAL MEMORANDA—Continued.

Year.	JULY.					AUGUST.					SEPTEMBER.				
	Highest.	Lowest.	Average Maxima.	Average Minama.	Mean Value.	Highest.	Lowest.	Average Maxima.	Average Minama.	Mean Value.	Highest.	Lowest.	Average Maxima.	Average Minama.	Mean Value.
1872	91.5	77.0	87.90	80.00	83.85	92.0	77.0	88.70	80.24	84.45	89.5	70.0	85 60	77.40	81.50
1873	98.0	70.0	90.48	76.66	83.57	92.5	71.0	88.33	75.74	82.28	91.0	65.0	85 48	73.65	79.56
1874	95.0	71.0	88.95	75.70	82.33	99.0	73.0	92.19	77.85	85.03	90.5	[illegible]1.5	86.86	73.97	80.41
1875															
M'n.			89.11	77.45	83.25			89.74	77.94	83.32			85.98	75.01	80.49

	OCTOBER.					NOVEMBER.					DECEMBER.					Year.
1872	80.0	59.9	73.40	66.40	69.85	74 0	38.0	62 93	54.98	58.93	74.0	21.0	57.80	48.90	53.35	71.99
1883	88.0	38.0	75.71	60.71	68.21	77.0	37.5	66.55	54.37	61 46	78 0	32.0	63.00	50 84	56.92	69.01
1874	87.0	51.0	78.60	63.29	70.94	83.5	41.[illegible]	71.08	57.13	64 10	78.5	42.0	66.18	52.69	59.43	71.01
1875																66.22
M'n.			75.90	63.47	69.67			66.85	55.49	61 50			62.33	50 81	56 57	69.71

Wheeler & Wilson

NEW IMPROVED

Sewing Machine,

The best Sewing Machine for Family, Plantation, Manufacturing and general work ever offered. Years have been spent in improving this machine, until it now stands before the world the

Only Really Perfect Sewing Machine.

Ladies should call and examine this

Family Favorite!

Which has stood the test of TWENTY-TWO YEARS of the most bitter opposition.

OFFICIAL AND RELIABLE STATISTICS,

Showing the contrast between the Wheeler & Wilson and other FAMILY SEWING MACHINES in use:

Wheeler & Wilson Family Machines	**1,325,666**
Singer Family Machines	995,125
Howe	631,020
Grover & Baker Family Machines	275,999
Weed Family Machines	199,876
Wilcox Gibbs Family Machines	103,222

Office and Sales-Room:

149 Canal Street, - - - - NEW ORLEANS, LA.

M. A. PECK,

Agent for Frank Leslie's Cut PAPER PATTERNS.

LOUIS GRUNEWALD,

Importer of

Musical Instruments,

Agent for the

PIANOS		ORGANS
OF		OF
Steinway		Mason & Hamlin,
KNABE,		
Haines,		Trayser & Co., (Stuttgart)
PLEYEL,		CHRISTOPHE, (Paris)
Wostermeyer.		

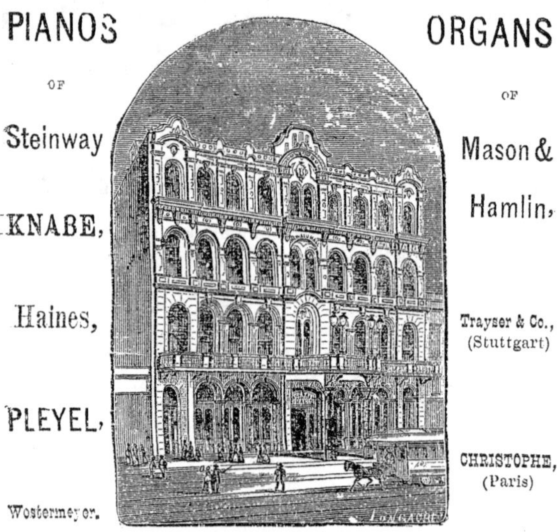

GRUNEWALD HALL,

16, 18, 20, 22, Baronne St., near Canal.

The only wholesale Music House South.

☞ Price lists sent on application.

METEOROLOGICAL MEMORANDA.

Record of Rain-Fall, Relative Humidity, the Occurrence of Frost, etc., for the Three Years Commencing July 1st, 1872, and Ending June 30th, 1874:

Year.	JANUARY.				FEBRUARY.				MARCH.			
	Rain-fall, inches.	No. of rainy days.	No.d'ys wh'n frost occ'd.	Relative Humidity.	Rain-fall, inches.	No. of rainy days.	No.d'ys wh'n frost occ'd.	Relative Humidity.	Rain-fall, inches.	No. of rainy days.	No.dy's wh'n frost occ'd.	Relative Humidity.
1872												
1873	5.04	7	1	76.80	2.20	6	1	73.49	5.54	10	2	74.03
1874	1.87	6	3	75.37	2.75	7	2	78.43	8 13	13	0	78.59
1875	7.43	16	1	77 51	13.25	8	4	69.93	11.81	11	1	70.20
M'n.	4.78	9.67	1.67	76.56	6 07	7	2.33	73.95	8.49	11.33	1	74.27

Year.	APRIL.				MAY.				JUNE.			
1872												
1873	1.38	3	0	69.03	21.87	16	0	78.25	7.36	16	0	79.00
1874	14.58	12	0	75.55	.12	1	0	65.41	8.97	10	0	71.83
1875	7,68	8	1	64.90	2.92	6	0	67.10	4.74	11	0	69,50
M'n.	7.88	7,67	.33	69.83	8 30	7 67	0	70.25	7.02	12,33	0	73,44

METEOROLOGICAL MEMORANDA—Continued.

Year.	JULY. Rain-fall, inches.	No. of rainy days.	No. d'ys wh'n frost occ'd.	Relative Humidity.	AUGUST. Rain-fall, inches.	No. of rainy days.	No. d'ys wh'n frost occ'd.	Relative Humidity.	SEPTEMBER. Rain-fall, inches.	No. of rainy days.	No. d'ys wh'n frost occ'd.	Relative Humidity.	Year—Total. Rain-fall.	Average Humidity.	Rainy days.	Frosts.
1872	5.09	14	0	77.60	3.35	10	0	75.00	1.99	5	0	72.50				
1873	7.43	17	0	73.94	10.46	14	0	78.50	3.27	10	0	77.46				
1874	11.74	14	0	74.08	4.65	11	0	70.78	2.47	8	0	70.60				
1875																
M'n.	8.09	15	0	75.21	6 15	11.67	0	74.76	2 58	7.67	0	73.52				
	OCTOBER.				NOVEMBER.				DECEMBER.							
1872	2.72	8	0	76.00	6.87	7	3	78.93	4 52	6	3	82 80	24.54	77.14	50	6
1873	1.43	4	1	72.10	7.77	8	1	75.34	1.38	6	4	77.07	75.13	75.40	117	0
1874	0	0	0	62.22	.69	3	4	73.78	3.31	11	2	76.92	59.28	72.80	96	1
1875													47.83	73.05	60	7
M'n.	1.38	4.00	.33	70.11	5.11	6.00	2.67	76.02	3.07	7.67	3.00	78.93	68.92	74.43	107	1

METEOROLOGICAL REMARKS—BAROMETER.

Annual average, 30.075 inches; Maximum, 30.60; Minimum, 29.60. The annual extreme between the maximum and minimum of pressure is about one inch.

EARLY AND LATE FROSTS.

Winter ol 1872 and 1873—First frost occurred on the morning of November 19th. 1872; the latest on March 6th, 1873.

Winter of 1873 and 1874—First frost occurred on October 30th; latest on February 9th.

Winter of 1874 and 1875—First frost occurred on November 1st; latest on April 3d.

RAIN-FALL.

Exceptionally heavy rains occurred on May 5th, 1873, measuring eight inches; on November 4th and 5th, 1873, nearly five inches; on July 3d and 4th, 1874, measuring nearly nine inches; and on February 15th to 18th, 1875, measuring nearly eight inches.

The greatest precipitation in the minimum space of time, occurred on May 5th, 1873, being eight inches in about four hours.

TEMPERATURE.

Average annual temperature, 69.71, F. The maximum temperature occurred on August 13th, 1874, being 99, F. The minimum on December 27th, being 21, F.

The greatest variation occurred on March 25th, 1873, the temperature descending from 80 F., at 2 o'clock, P. M., to 43, F., at 12 P. M., being 37 degrees. The average temperature for the months of March, April and May is 69.20, F.; for June, July and August, 82.63, F.; for September, October and November, 70.55, F.; and for December, January and February, 56.12, F.

The foregoing memoranda were obtained from the records of the Board of Health for the three years, July 1st, 1872, to June 30th, 1875, inclusive.

From the records of a series of observations made at Jackson Barracks, below the city of New Orleans, from

1856 to 1860, the following additional data were obtained: Annual average temperature, 69.94, F.; maximum, 97, F.; minimum, 31.75, F.

In the series of years 1822 to 1854, the highest temperature recorded was 100 F., and the lowest, 8 F., in January, 1852. In five of these thirty-two years the temperature descended below 25 F., in three of these below 20. Thus the extremes of this climate may be considered as from 25 to 100 degrees.

There appears to have been no material difference in temperature between these periods anterior and those given subsequent to the war, but a very marked contrast in the amount of annual rain-fall. In records of measurements for different series of many years, as published in Blodget's Climatology of the United States, the average annual precipitation is given at about fifty-one inches, while the records above published show an annual average for the past three years of nearly 70 inches.

We are indebted to Dr. S. E. Chaillé. Professor of Physiology and Pathological Anatomy, Medical Department University of Louisiana, for the following article on the

HEALTH OF NEW ORLEANS.

On this subject there has been much exaggeration, both at home and abroad; residents being prone to claim a too favorable, and strangers to fear and credit a too unfavorable condition. Facts from official reports are alone trustworthy, and some of these will be briefly stated.

This city has been grievously afflicted with yellow fever. It is doubtful if during any one of the last eighty years—1796 to 1876—New Orleans has been entirely exempt from cases of this disease. During the sixty-three years, 1796 to 1859, it was ravaged by thirty-four serious epidemics; but during the past seventeen years, 1859 to 1876, there has been but one epidemic, that of 1867, and during the other sixteen of these years the annual number of deaths has been insignificant. Thus, this special enemy has apparently expended its strength. When present, its ravages are committed in July, August, September and October; during the remaining eight months none need fear it. To the prevalence in the past of this disease is chiefly due the evil sanitary reputation of New Orleans. Such is the terror inspired by it that its fatality is greatly over estimated, and its presence, even in a single case, gives rise to the most extravagant reports, which represent the fears of the timid and ignorant, rather than the facts, and which, repeated by newspapers greedy for sensational items, inflict annually on this city serious injury, and tend to perpetuate an ill repute which the facts have ceased to justify.

Malaria has also been an enemy to New Orleans; but in recent years malarial fevers have been generally of mild type, due, no doubt, to the gradually improving drainage, They prevail chiefly during the same months as yellow fever, and will so continue until such time as a more perfect drainage shall free the city from them forever.

Official statistics show that during the past ten years the annual death rate has averaged about thirty deaths to every one thousand population—the still births and deaths by epidemics being excluded. The death rate for the eight months—November to July—is much less than 30 per 1000, comparing advantageously with other large cities. The first four months of the year—January to April—represent the most healthy season, during which life and health are as secure as in the most favored cities of the world.

PLACES OF AMUSEMENT.

ACADEMY OF MUSIC.

Deservedly is this place of amusement popular with all who find themselves "within our gates." Its name is never mentioned by our citizens except with a smile and expectations of pleasure, and especially is this so with ladies and children, to whom the "Academy Matinees" are always enjoyable events.

The building was erected in 1853, by George C. Lawrason, Esq., for its present proprietor, Mr. David Bidwell, and was opened as an amphitheatre by the well known circus man, Dan Rice.

In 1854 it was changed to a regular theatre, and as such has held a front rank ever since. The interior arrangements are admirable. Neat and convenient reception and dressing rooms are provided for ladies and children. An elaborate steam apparatus supplies the auditorium with hot or cold air, according to the season. The seats are comfortable and the decorations elegant and attractive. Every arrangement has been made for the safety and comfort of guests.

Mr. Bidwell takes great pride in the profession, and superintends in person the entire business of his theatre.

A series of entertainments are given which embrace the leading artists in all departments of the histrionic art, presenting a round of amusements which never fail to draw crowded houses, and give entire satisfaction to the patrons of the theatre. From the arrangements made, we have no doubt the present season will be one of the most brilliant ever known in the history of the Academy, and a visit there cannot fail to be productive of much pleasure and enjoyment.

VARIETIES THEATRE.

This gem of a theatre, on the north side of Canal street, between Dauphine and Burgundy, is the successor of the famed old Gaioty, afterwards Variety Theatre, which was situated on Gravier, between Carondelet and Baronne, where the elegant building of the New Orleans Cotton Exchange now stands. The old Variety was destroyed by fire in 1854, and again a few years ago, when the Association concluded to locate their new building in a more prominent position. The present site was selected, and soon the New Varieties Theatre sprang into existence.

This association, formed of the leading men of New Orleans, has spared no expense in the construction of this favorite place of amusement, which is elegant and complete in all its appointments, and has the finest entrance of any theatre on the Continent. The Gaiety, under the management of the genial Tom Placide, gained an extensive and enviable reputation, and it would seem as if the New Varieties, was to rival its predecessor in this respect, as it has, so far, been particularly favored in its representations and management. Mr. Tayleure and Mrs. Chaufrau are the lessees and managers for the coming winter. The fame and world-wide reputation and unbounded success of these artists, are sufficient guarantees that this will be a season of unprecedented attractions and consequent popularity.

ST. CHARLES THEATRE,

St. Charles street, between Commercial Place and Poydras street, is an old time landmark, and favorite with the people of New Orleans. It is a spacious and commodious building, well arranged, and has a national reputation as an histrionic temple.

THE OPERA HOUSE.

This spacious structure was erected in 1859, under the auspices of the Opera House Company.

It is situated on the corner of Bourbon and Toulouse streets, having a very elegant front on the former, and is considered one of the finest buildings of the sort in the United States.

The interior is arranged and supplied with all the care and conveniences required in a first class Temple of the Muses, the spacious stage, and scenic apparatus being particularly appreciated and noted by artists and visitors.

We very much regret to say that there will be no regular opera troupe this winter.

GLOBE THEATRE.

This building, corner of Perdido and Baronne streets, was built with the intention of having the drama interpreted in the German language on its stage, but circumstances proving adverse, it has been let for various purposes from time to time, and is at present used for variety performances.

HOME INDUSTRIES.

Until within the past few years, we have done very little in manufacturing goods or articles for home consumption, relying upon the products of our fertile soil and genial climate for the sources of wealth and prosperity. Lately, however, much attention has been given to the manufacture of many articles of necessity, ornament or luxury, and ere many years we shall, no doubt, hear the busy hum of thousands of operatives in every branch of this most desirable adjunct to the commercial power of a city. Among the most important of these factories, we may mention the extensive soap works of

J. H. KELLER,

located on Front, between Josephine and St. Andrew streets. The history of this enterprising and liberal minded merchant is an encouraging example of the esults which may be accomplished by perseverance, industry and unswerving integrity. Mr. Keller commenced business as a manufacturer of soaps in 1849. Previously all good soap for the wholesale trade was imported from the North and Europe, and thus many hundred thousands of dollars were taken from our city. Mr. Keller commenced in a small way; his first year's business amounting to only two thousand boxes, and considering the competition he was obliged to meet, it will be readily believed that his profits were not large. But he was not a man to be frightened by obstacles; he made a good article, gave good weight, kept his expenses low, and was satisfied to make a living. He had not entered the lists with the expectation of amassing a fortune, but with the determination of making a business which would constantly increase, and give satisfaction to his customers as well as himself. His enterprise made a market for

SPORTSMEN'S DEPOT.

RICHARD RHODES,

(Late F. Charleville,)

NO. 55 St. Charles Street,

Guns, Rifles, Revolvers,

Game Bags, Shot Pouches, Flasks, etc.,

RODS, NETS, LINES, ETC.,

All articles required for Hunting and Fishing, at

MODERATE PRICES.

Supply Yourself with a Copy of

NEW ORLEANS

CITY DIRECTORY

FOR 1876,

Containing a Map of the City and Street Guide.

L. SOARDS & CO.,

Publishers, 5 Commercial Place.

many tons annually of fatty matter, which before had been wasted, and gave employment to a large number of people.

The reputation of Keller's soap stands second to none in the country, and the demand has been growing year by year, until last year his sales went over sixty thousand boxes, and the wide spread popularity of his brands necessitated an enlargement of his establishment and additional facilities.

For this purpose he has just erected a splendid building having a front of one hundred and fifty-five feet on Freret street, with two wings fronting on Josephine and St. Andrew streets, which are each two hundred and thirty-one feet long, all fire-proof. In this splendid structure he has three enormous kettles; the first has a capacity of twenty-two thousand gallons, and in it one hundred and eighty thousand pounds of soap may be finished; The next kettle holds fourteen thousand gallons, and one hundred and ten thousand pounds of soap may be finished from it, and the other kettle has a capacity of four thousand gallons, or thirty-five thousand pounds of soap. Besides these he has several kettles of smaller dimensions. The establishment is fitted up with all the latest and most approved machinery, the whole giving Mr. Keller such facilities that he can now double the quantity produced last year, and sell soap as cheap as anywhere in the world.

Mr. Keller is just about to add the toilet soap making to the line of his manufactures, and expects to turn out as fine an article as any in the country.

The importation of boots and shoes has been an immense trade, but of late years many of our business men have embarked in the manufacture of these articles, and among them

JOHN HANSEN,

No. 35 Canal, corner of Peters street, is one of the most active and energetic. Mr. Hansen has recently enlarged his factory, employing a large force of experienced and skillful workmen, and is now turning out all descriptions of boots and shoes of a quality superior to Northern-made articles, and at prices which makes the competition practical, and must lead to a constantly increasing trade. Mr. Hansen, upon commencing his present factory, made a strong appeal to our people to support him in his efforts to give employment to the deserving by manufacturing at home, and we are pleased to know that the response has been such as to encourage him to make still greater improvements. Twenty-five years' experience in the business, during which he has worked with a persistent industry, has given Mr. Hansen the knowledge necessary for the successful prosecution of his business, and make it an important adjunct to the trade of our city.

A decided improvement in the

TEA AND COFFEE

trade has been made by Mr. J. J. Martin, No. 5 Camp street. Besides the immense business that he does in tea of all grades and prices, he has recently introduced steam into his establishment, which is used in parching and grinding the great quantities of coffee which he sells. One of the novelties of Camp street, which cannot fail to attract the attention of strangers, is the great coffee pot on the gallery of his store, which may be seen steaming away at all hours of the day.

P. H. HARMON

has for years been engaged in the manufacture of brooms, an article of every day use, which formerly came almost entirely from the North and West. Having had long experience in the business, Mr. Harmon secured the most approved machinery and a number of skilled workmen, and at once entered into competition with these older manufacturers. So successful has he been that almost the entire trade of this section is now supplied with brooms manufactured in this city. Mr. Harmon's factory is at No. 96 Tchoupitoulas street

A novelty in

SEWING MACHINES

may be seen at the establishment of Mr. Wm. Gregg, No. 154 Canal street. This is a sewing machine run by steam, and thousands of persons, as they pass, stop to inspect this wonderful instrument. Mr. Gregg has sold a number of these machines, and all have given the most entire satisfaction to their purchasers.

About six months ago

JOHN KENZ

commenced the manufacture of boots and shoes at No. 16 Royal street, in the building known as the Old Post Office. He has already gained a wide reputation for furnishing good, durable and cheap articles. Besides making boots and shoes to supply his own store and to sell to the trade, Mr. Kenz takes orders, and at short notice will supply a home made article, neat, stylish and comfortable. He makes shoes at from $3 50 upwards, and sells at wholesale and retail. The patronage recieved by those engaged in this important branch of trade will cause them to increase their facilities, and thus a large amount of money formerly sent abroad will be kept here to encourage the mechanics and laborers of our own city.

In this connection we desire to call attention to the

SASH AND BLIND FACTORY

of Mr. George Purves, located at the corner of St. Charles and Clio streets. This factory is supplied with all the latest machinery, and turns out work equal to any in the world. Mr. Purves now supplies much of the sash, blinds and doors, dressed lumber, etc., which formerly came from the West, and prides himself that he can compete, not only in quality and style, but in prices, with all foreign manufacturers.

PUBLIC BUILDINGS.

THE CUSTOM HOUSE.

Thirty years ago the First Municipality of New Orleans offered the United States its choice of several squares, to be conveyed in fee simple, provided a Custom House, worthy of the growing commerce of the city would be erected. The United States accepting the proposition, the Secretary of the Treasury, selected the "Custom House Square" as the most eligible of those offered, and in a short time thereafter the plans of A. T. Wood were adopted, November 22d, 1847, and the work commenced October 23, 1848. A thirty years' review of how the work has been conducted on this St. Peters of New Orleans, would be altogether incompatable with the space or business of a guide book ; suffice it that the work *was* carried on with greater or less expedition, according to the means at disposal, till the war, when, for a time, it was entirely suspended. When work was recommenced, under Colonel Morse, the building was literally filled with rubbish of all sorts, To remove this and finish the portion now used as the Post Office was the first task of this gentleman and his skilled assistants. How well they have performed their labors can easily be seen by a visit to the building. Next the completion of the

BUSINESS ROOM

engrossed their attention.

A glance at this beautiful room, *the finest business room in the world*, is all that we can give. The size of the entire room is 125x95 feet ; the height—from floor to glass dome or ceiling, fifty-four feet. Fourteen lofty columns are placed so as to give the central part of the room, a space of 45x65 feet, for the use of the general public, and outside that for the accommodation of the officers and clerks. The columns are of the Corinthian order with attic bases ; the lower portion of the shaft plain and polished. the capital varied to allow of designs indicative of the purposes of the room. At the top of each capital is a basso relievo of Juno, and another of Mercury, and designs of cotton and tobacco plants. These are so arranged that each faces its opposite on every column, and by looking at four capitals from any position, all the designs can be comprehended at a glance. The tiling of the floor is laid out, in pattern, of black and white marble, in tiles, each two feet square, with borders in black marble from column to column. Sixteen light holes are cut in the floor, four feet six inches in diameter, floored with glass one inch thick, cast on a hammered surface to break the rays of light, and which will be ground to a smooth surface, when it will present the appearance of green marble. Each plate is the centre of a star, handsomely inlaid of black marble. The room is heated by steam, the steam coils being suspended in the floor from the arches, and shielded by hexegon pedestals with marble tops.

Altogether, the room is a wonderful triumph of the art and genius of man, and must be seen to be understood or appreciated.

To Mr. John J. Hannan, the skilled Superintendent, much praise is deservedly given for the able manner in which he has conducted the finishing of the Post Office department of the building, as also the work done on the magnificent room which is the subject of our sketch.

STATE HOUSE.

Formerly known throughout the country as the St. Louis Hotel, was built in 1841, and was for many years one of the most famous hotels in the South. It was within the walls of this magnificent structure that the people of New Orleans entertained Henry Clay in the winter of 1842, in a style commensurate with the wealth and refinement of the then prosperous and hopeful Crescent City, and in its famous ball room, the Convention to frame a new State Constitution met in 1843, which embraced almost every man of influence and talent in

Louisiana. John R. Grimes, Pierre Soulé, Christian Roselius, Roman, Downs, Eustis, Brent, Marigny, Conrad, and such other distinguished gentlemen, scholars, statesmen and patriots. While its elegant rotunda was used as a Chamber of Commerce, Board of Brokers and Cotton Exchange room, as well as for the political meetngs of the Whig and Democratic parties, or for those of charitable or other purposes. This time-honored building, around which so many ennobling and pleasing memories cluster, has for the past two years been used as a State House. The building is on St. Louis street, between Chartres and Royal.

CITY HALL.

Corner of St. Charles and Layfayette streets, contains the different municipal business rooms, Treasurer's office, Lyceum and Library, etc., and is a large, commodeous and handsome structure of brick, marble and stone. The front is of the Grecian Doric order and remarkable for the graceful beauty of its stately columns.

ODD FELLOW'S HALL.

This building, on Camp between Lafayette and Poydras, is, as its name indicates, the temple of the I. O. O. F. in our city, and is of national fame on account of its use and for the many brilliant assemblages that have graced its spacious and beautifully finished ball room. The lodge rooms are said to be without equals for arrangements and appointments, and this rapidly increasing Order may well congratulate itself on giving to New Orleans one of the chief ornaments among her public buildings.

NEW MASONIC HALL.

This building of which the foundation and corner stone alone are laid, will, when completed, be one of the finest and most beautiful in our city. It will front on St. Charles street, just above Tivoli Circle, and be of large dimensions, having a front of 147 feet, depth 92 feet, and two wings 38 feet wide by 84 feet deep.

The corner stone was laid on February 15, 1872, with all the solemn and imposing rites of Masonic ceremonies. It is a beautiful block of granite from the mountains of Georgia, and a present from the Grand Lodge of that State. The Masonic grand bodies and many of the lodges occupy the old Masonsic Hall on St. Charles street, opposite Commercial Place.

THE CITY PRISONS.

These edifices, which are three stories high and built of brick, at a cost of about $200,000, are situated between St. Ann and Orleans streets, occupying 123 feet on each and a space of 139 feet between them. They are two in number, divided by a wide passage way. The main building has its principal entrance on Orleans street, which is closed by strong iron doors. The lower story is used as offices and apartments of the jailor. The second and third stories are used for prisoners, and are divided into large rooms. The building is surmounted by a pavillion with an alarm bell.

ST. PATRICK'S HALL.

This stately edifice, corner of Camp and Lafayette streets, built for the St. Patrick's Hall Association, has been recently added to the fine buildings of our city, the corner stone being laid March 17, 1874. The building, which is the result of the energy and public spirit of a few well known citizens, is one of the most elegant and spacious in the South, and is justly a matter of pride to the projectors of the enterprise. The lofty and spacious concert room is one of the finest in the United States, and has already achieved an extensive fame for the magnitude and beauty of its proportions.

GRUNEWALD HALL.

This edifice, although the result of the private enterprise and personal energy of the gentleman whose name it bears, may still be justly classed among the finest of our public buildings. It is a handsome four story stone front structure, situated on Baronne street, between Canal and Common streets, having a front on Baronne street of 103 feet by a depth of 160 feet.

The graceful proportions and admirable arrangements throughout reflect the highest credit upon the refined taste and good judgment of this public spirited citizen.

The lower story is occupied by the owner of the building, Mr. Louis Grunewald, as a music store and show rooms for musical instruments, and are the most spacious and elegantly fitted up of the sort in the South. The other stories, which contain many large, airy and lofty rooms, are occupied as club rooms, offices, etc.

On the second floor is the now famous concert hall, 100 by 54 feet, one of the most magnificent in point of construction and ornamentation to be found anywhere. The very perfect acoustics of the room make it a favorite auditorium with our music loving population, and an appreciated stage by professional and amateur singers. While in this city, that queen of song, M'lle Ilma de Murska, repeatedly praised the acoustics of the Grunewald Concert Hall, pronouncing it the most perfect for the transmission of sounds that she had ever sang in. The central position of the Hall gives it prominence as regards convenience of access by dwellers in all parts of New Orleans, as well as sojourners in our principal hotels and boarding houses.

EXPOSITION BUILDING.

This elegant building, situated between Julia and Girod streets, having a front of 85 feet on both St. Charles and Carondelet streets, running through the square by straight lines 341 feet. Besides other large well finished rooms for various purposes, it has a concert hall 170x81, with a 41 foot ceiling, in which King of the Carnival gives his receptions and balls on Mardi Gras. This is decidedly the handsomest room of the kind in the South.

MECHANICS' INSTITUTE.

This substantial and stately building is on the east side of Dryades street, near Canal, and is one of the finest in the city. On the lower floor is the library and committee room of the New Orleans Mechanics' Society. It was in this edifice that the State Senate and House of Representatives met previous to the selection of the St. Louis Hotel as the State House.

Wheeler & Wilson

NEW IMPROVED

Sewing Machine,

The best Sewing Machine for Family, Plantation, Manufacturing and general work ever offered. Years have been spent in improving this machine, until it now stands before the world the

Only Really Perfect Sewing Machine.

Ladies should call and examine this

Family Favorite!

Which has stood the test of TWENTY-TWO YEARS of the most bitter opposition.

OFFICIAL AND RELIABLE STATISTICS,

Showing the contrast between the Wheeler & Wilson and other FAMILY SEWING MACHINES in use:

Wheeler & Wilson Family Machines	**1,325,666**
Singer Family Machines	995,125
Howe	631,020
Grover & Bnker Family Machines	275,999
Weed Family Machines	199,876
Wilcox & Gibbs Family Machines	103,222

Office and Sales-Room:

149 Canal Street, - - - - NEW ORLEANS, LA.

M. A. PECK,

Agent for Frank Leslie's Cut PAPER PATTERNS.

NEW ORLEANS GAS WORKS.

The first gas used in this city was in the Camp Street Theatre, owned by the late James H. Caldwell, to whose energy and enterprise New Orleans is much indebted. The first gas company was formed in 1829, but did not succeed, and gas was not regularly introduced into the city until 1834, when by Mr. Caldwell's efforts a company was formed, which has ever since been one of the most prosperous corporations of our city.

The works, which are said to be the best constructed of their kind in this country, are about a mile from the river, and occupy the whole of the square bounded by Gravier, Perdido, Magnolia and Locust streets.

The offices of the company are in the elegant building corner of Common and Baronne streets, one of the most costly and showy structures of which our city can boaot.

MORESQUE BUILDING.

This magnificent iron building occupies a small square bounded by Poydras, North, Camp and St. Mary's, 150 feet on each street. The edifice is three stories and an attic in height. The four fronts are of iron, in the Moorish style, and were made at the foundry of McElvain & Co., Holly Springs, Mississippi. This splendid property is owned by the heirs of the late John Gauche Esq.

NEW ORLEANS SAVINGS INSTITUTION.

This handsome bank, 156 Canal street, is one of the most elegant business houses in the South, whether the dimensions, the convenience, or beauty of finish be considered. The massive carved furniture and richly frescoed walls of the interior are master works of art, and well worthy of inspection.

MINERVA HALL.

This handsome little hall is situated on Clio, between Prytania and St. Charles streets. It was for many years under charge of the late Prof. Vegas, who made it a popular place for private parties, balls. soirees, ladies' fairs and other entertainments. It is now under charge of Prof. Auguste Davis, whose musical compositions have obtained a national reputation. Prof. Davis has here a large dancing class, numbering many of the best people of our city. The hall is still rented for private parties, balls, etc., and its convenient location, accessible by city railroads, makes it a general favorite for such purposes.

SOCIETIES.

HOWARD ASSOCIATION.

This society, which was organized in August 1837, has always held a foremost rank among the benevolent Associations of New Orleans. During seasons of health and prosperity it is seldom heard of, but when pestilence and want stalk abroad, the members buckle on their armor, and with a self-abnegation well worthy of the memory of the great English philanthropist from whom the society takes its name, go forth to relieve the suffering and distress of their fellow beings, making no distinction on account of wealth or position in their ministrations.

The present officers of the Association are; E. F. Schmidt, President; J. F. Vandergriff, Vice President; R. L. Robertson, Treasurer, and F. R. Southmayd, Secretary.

SHAKESPEARE CLUB.

This club which was organized on the 8th of May, 1867, is deservedly a favorite with the people of New Orleans. Originally organized by the members of the Louisiana Histrionics and Crescent Dramatic Association, its history as a dramatic association has been a series of brilliant successes, while its roll of non-acting members, numbering many of the most intelligent and estimable young men, and some of the staunchest of our merchants, gives it a standing as a social club, equal to any in the country.

The Shakespeares were, we believe, the first to introduce what is called "complimentary entertainments," the entire expenses being borne by the members, whose friends are invited to witness the performances, in the same spirit as an individual would select the company for a social gathering in his own parlors. It may therefore well be believed that their audiences include the most refined, intelligent and respected of our people, and make up assemblages of beauty and fashion rarely equaled. Among the plays presented, all of which were rendered with an excellence denoting careful study, correct appreciation and artistic ability of the highest order, we may mention, Richelieu, Ingomar, Love's Sacrifice, Marble Heart, Lady of Lyons, The Rivals, Macbeth, Hamlet, and Money. In fact the dramatic portfolio of the club has embraced all or nearly all of the really good plays of the day, in the production of which a versatality of talent has been displayed among its members, which could not be surpassed by any other similar organization in the country.

But the club, like all things human, has had its trials and misfortunes. The destruction of its beautiful Club House, corner Canal and Dryades streets, with all the furniture, books and other valuables, without insurance, threw upon it a financial load which would have extinguished almost any other society. But there were those among its members who were attached to the old fame, and who determined to fight their way through to prominence and prosperity again. Their object has at last been accomplished; the club is once more out of debt and established on a firm financial basis. For this result too much credit can not be given to the worthy President of the club, Col. W. T. Vaudry, who has administered its affairs for nearly three years with rare ability and judgment. By a course of firmness and justice, always combined with courtesy, he has held the members together, making the club still more a favorite with them, while his genial bearing and sterling qualities, both in social and business circles, have attracted to the club many of the best men of our city. In his efforts he has been well supported by Messrs. A. Hero, Jr., Dave C. Johnson, T. O'Neill, Frank H. Wilson, Judge Geo. H. Braughn, and other gentlemen, who are deservedly popular with all who know them, and are earnest workers in whatever cause they may espouse.

The club now occupies the splendid suite of rooms over the front of the Varieties Theatre, on Canal, be- Dauphine and Burgundy streets. The furniture is of the latest styles, and the walls are adorned with beautiful pictures and all the comforts of club life are provided for its members.

The present officers of the club are; W. T. Vaudry, President; A. W. Hyatt, Vice President; Andrew Hero, Jr., Financial Secretary; Joseph M. Payro, Treasurer Frank H. Wilson, Secretary; Ed. Lilienthal., F. H. Whiteker, E. C. Bullard, Stewards.

ORLEANS DRAMATIC ASSOCIATION.

This club, which was organized on June 30, 1866, has a splendid suite of rooms at the corner of St. Charles and Common streets, the entrance being on the first named thoroughfare. During the summer season they give to their friends and admirers a series of complimentary entertainments, which call together the representatives of the wealth, beauty and fashion of our city, presenting audiences of rare brilliancy. Their dramatic performances have always been characterized by good taste, skill and ability, the strength of the Association showing marked talent in every department of the histrionic art. During the visit of the Knights Templar, the Association, by their prompt action in receiving and entertaining our guests, well maintained the reputation of New Orleans for generous hospitality. They have, in their many entertainments, appeared in nearly all the leading society plays and dramas, attaining a degree of excellence in each which might well be referred to with pride by their friends.

The present officers of the Association are: John J. Miller, President; W. H. Beanham, Vice President; Frank M. Kerr, Recording Secretary; Thomas A. Gleason, Corresponding Secretary; Leon Meyers, Treasurer; E. J. Angell, Financial Secretary; Geo. Stern, Stage Manager; John A. Cairnes, Assistant Stage Manager.

CRESCENT CITY RIFLE CLUB.

Among the pastimes to which the gentlemen of our city devote their leisure hours, none is more popular than that of rifle shooting. Some time last spring a number of the admirers of this sport, wishing to have a place where long range practicing could be had, resolved to form a new Rifle Club, and from this resolution sprang the Association whose name heads this article. The charter is dated 31st July, 1875, and recorded on the 21st of September following, the original being signed by the following well known and popular gentlemen: William J. Behan, W. T. Vaudry, John Glynn, Jr., Wm. H. Renaud, Samuel Muller, R. M. Fauquier and James Buckley.

With their usual promptness and energy these gentlemen proceeded with the work of organization, securing and fitting up a park. The ground selected is on Bayou St. John, just beyond the long bridge, where ample room for any desired range was found. Here a handsome Club House has been built and supplied with all appurtenances for the enjoyment of this invigorating and healthful sport.

The Club has three batteries, two hundred, five hundred and one thousand yards each, the position of the batteries being well chosen, so as to give to the marksmen the best possible light for good practice. The park was formerly a plantation, one of the first under cultivation in our State. A legend is told to the effect that its ancient owner, to secure his treasures from the prying eyes of the world, buried a fabulous sum of gold, in a leather trunk, among the grand old cedars which fill the park on the left of the Club House. Whether this be true or not, the cedars are there, ranged in rows, and interspersed with full grown orange trees, making delightfully shaded avenues, just the place for a family pic-nic, or a quiet ramble in *good* company.

"Round and round the rowan tree, out upon the green,
Darting here and there about, merry spirits are seen.
What is that to you or I? None the wiser we,
If fairy elf, or fairy fay, sport upon the lea,"

What a merry place this will be when the Club gives its festival! Myriads of lights hanging among the arches of those old trees, the sweet perfume of orange blossoms, mingling with that from a thousand other flowers, charming ladies and gallant men, music, laughter and gay conversation—all that is required by the cultivated and refined for real enjoyment. Our visitors should not fail to take a trip to this delighful sylvan retreat where they sre certain to be courteously received.

The officers of the Club are Col. W. J. Behan, President; Col. W. T. Vaudry, Vice President; Samuel Mullen, Secretary, and John K. Renaud, Treasurer. Trustees—W. H. Renaud, Col. John Glynn, Jr., Col. M. Buck Miller, Capt. A. C. Smith, and Dr. Geo. Howe. Shooting masters—Maj. F. O. Minor, G. R. Ober, Dudley Selph, Maj. Wm. Arms. Armorer—Wm. Weiss.

No spirituous or malt liquors are allowed on the grounds, and all betting is strictly prohibited.

The club now numbers about two hundred members, among whom are some gentlemen who have been prominent as riflemen for twenty-five years. Wednesday and Sunday are practice days, and on either of these days some excellent shooting may be witnessed.

NEW ORLEANS TYPOGRAPHICAL UNION.

Formed May 9, 1835. Reorganized under the National charter. One of the most flourishing Unions in the country, having at present a membership of about 350. Rooms corner Perdido and Carondelet streets.

Officers: E. Bentley, President; J. C. Murray, Vice President; Geo. C. Crowther, Recording Secretary; J C. Rollins, Corresponding Secretary; W. H. Drury, Financial Secretary; T. F. Hedges, Treasurer.

CLERK'S BENEVOLENT ASSOCIATION.

This Association was organized in 1865, and has become one of the most popular societies in our city. Combining benevolence with pleasant social intercourse, it has relieved its sick members, assisted those looking for employment, and every year enlarged its sphere of usefulness.

The officers at present are as follows: John. C. Smith, President; E. A. Louis, Vice President; A. Lasalle, Treasurer; Geo. W. Emanuel, Recording Secretary; Henry Durel, Jr., Financial Secretary; L. L. Knapp, Grand Conductor; F. Camba, Assistant Conductor; J.

C. Wilder, Guardian, and C. F. Schnell, Aug. B. Diemel, P. Tisné, Jr., Charles Oberle, F. A. Thiel, R. M. Hailes, A. H. C. Odenwald and Joseph Garcia, Board of Directors.

YOUNG MEN'S BENEVOLENT ASSOCIATION.

Rooms, Grunewald Hall. Geo. H. Braughn, President; Eug. Lalmant, Vice President; S. Suter, Treasurer; J. J. Bercejay, Secretary.

AURORA BENEVOLENT ASSOCIATION.

Organized May 1st, 1872. Meets first and third Friday of each month. Hall corner of Exchange Alley and Custom House street.

Officers: Eugene May, President; A. F. McLain, Vice President; A. Kalinski, Treasurer; Edgar L. Mahen, Recording Secretary; J. A. C. Wadsworth, Financial Secretary; John J. Mellon, Grand Marshal; J. O. Jackson, Grand Conductor; A. Smith, Inside Sentinal.

CATHOLIC TOTAL ABSTINENCE.

State Union.—Officers :: Rev. D. McKiniry, Spiritual Director; Thos. G. Rapier, President; H. R. Giffney, First Vice President; J. T. A. O'Meallie, Second Vice President; J. C. M. Kavenaugh, Secretary; William H. Byrnes, Grand Marshal; P. J. Donnegan, Sergeant-at Arms.

MASONIC.

Qfficers of the Grand Lodge: John G. Fleming. Grand Master; Wm. Robson, Deputy Grand Master; Wm. R. Whitaker, Senior Grand Warden; Julius Lisso, Junior Grand Warden; A. W. Hyatt, Grand Treasurer; Jas. C. Batchelor, M. D., Grand Secretary.

There are 32 lodges in the city.

The officers of the Grand Chapter of

ROYAL ARCH MASONS.

Samuel J. Powell, Grand High Priest; Jos. H. DeGrange, Deputy Grand High Priest; Jas. C. Batchelor, Grand Secretary.

OFFICERS OF GRAND COUNCIL.

W. R. Whitaker, M. P. Grand Master; C. B. Wheeler,

Deputy J. Grand Master; Gustave Sontag, Grand Recorder.

Officers Grand Commandry

KNIGHTS TEMPLAR.

Sir Jos. H. DeGrange, R. E. Grand Commander; Sir M. E. Girard, V. E. D. Grand Commander; Sir Gustave Sontag, E. Grand Recorder.

Officers of the Grand Consistory

32D DEGREE, A. AND A. S. R.

J. B. Scott, Grand Commander-in-Chief; Gustave Sontag, Grand Recorder.

ODD FELLOWS.

Officers of the Grand Lodge: S. B. Sifers. M. W. Grand Master; Wm. Seymour, R. W. D. Grand Master; A. J. Vandegriff, R. W. Grand Warden; F. W. Delesdernier. R. W. Grand Secretary; Jno. B. Heno, R. W. Grand Treasurer; W. C. Wilson, S. T. Grisamore, R. W. Grand Representatives to G. L. U. S; J. G. Dunlap, W. Grand Chaplin; C. Ellerman, W. Grand Marshal; H. Feiman, W. Grand Conductor; J. Potter', W. Grand Guardian; G. F. Mathes, W. Grand Herald.

There are 24 lodges in the State, 14 of which are in the city.

SEVEN WISE MEN,

Officers Grand Conclave of Louisiana: G. W. Sniff, Grand Archon; F. Fuhr, Grand Chancellor; E. R. Boher, Grand Provost; Jas. Scheling, Grand Treasurer; W. S. Crockett, Grand Financial Scribe; A. Sambola, Grand Scribe; C. H. Hoffner, Grand Inspector General; H. Copple, Grand Herald; O. S. Babcock, Grand Prelate.

VARIETY DRAMATIC CLUB.

Club Room No. 16, St. Charles street. Officers: John M. Conway, President; William Gowland, Vice President; John R. Stewart, Recording Secretary; A. F. Michel, Financial Secretary; L. A. Davidson, Treasurer; Max Stern, Stage Manager.

Philip Werlein,

At the Old Stand,

Nos. 78, 80, 82 and 90 BARONNE STREET,

NEW ORLEANS,

Is supplying thousands of customers with Pianos, Organs, Music and Musical Instruments. Those who give the best value will and should do the leading trade.

All are invited to inspect mammoth stock of pianos,

CHICKERING'S, the best in the world,

DUNHAM'S, and J. P. HALE'S,

Organs :

ESTEY'S and NEEDHAM'S.

Second hand Pianos and Organs $50 and upwards.

This is the old reliable Southern Music House.

GARRICK CLUB.

Meetings held in Grunewald Hall.

Officers: Judge W. T. Houston, President; E. Lalmant, Vice President; Louis Richards, Secretary; S. G. Kreeger, Treasurer; E. A. Cowan, Stage Manager; Ben Onorato, Assistant Stage Manager.

SOUTHERN DRAMATIC CLUB.

Club Room No. 108, Canal street.

Officers: John B. Cefalu, President; L. J. Llambias, Vice President; T. R. Fox, Recording Secretary; L. Schwarz, Financial Secretary; Geo. C. Samuels, Treasurer; M. H. Redon, Stage Manager; A. J. Dalamare, Janitor.

NEW HISTRONIC DRAMATIC ASSOCIATION.

Club Room in Grunewald Hall.

Officers: Jos. H. Spearing, President; H. N. Copperwaithe, Vice President; Charles F. Pitts, Recording Secretary; W. J. Smith, Financial Secretary; B. J. O'Neil Treasurer; R. M. Hailes, Stage Manager.

ST. JOHN ROWING CLUB.

Boat House on Bayou St. John, near Bayou Bridge.
Officers: John Glynn, Jr., President; R. L. Macmurdo, Vice President; A. K. Brown, Secretary; L. W. Perkins, Treasurer; E. B. Musgrove, Captain, and F. W. Baker, G. H. Dunbar and H. Chalaron, Trustees.

PERSERVEANCE ROWING CLUB.

Boat House New Basin; near Magnolia Bridge.

In August last some of the lovers of aquatic sports organized this club, and without making any noise about the matter, proceeded to build and fit up a handsome club house at the place above stated. Among the leading spirits in the enterprise was Capt. John Fitzpatrick, whose genial and kindly manners make him a favorite with all who know him. He was ably assisted by Messrs. Rohders, Graham, Boyle, and others, and now the club numbers about sixty members, all made of the right stuff.

The officers are: F. Rohders, President; J. J. Kuhner,

Vice President; G. R. Graham, Secretary; J. Rohders, Treasurer; John Fitzpatrick, Captain, and Wm. Graham Lieutenant. The governing committee is composed of the above officers and Messrs. G. Biegel, P. Ziegler and Ed. Burke.

PELICAN ROWING CLUB.

Boat House Bayou St. John. Officers: John E. Bailey, President; E. E. Brugere, Secretary; Joseph H. Bayhi, Treasurer; Paul Chaudet, Captain.

NEW ORLEANS P ESS CLUB.

Organized May, 1875. Rooms No. 18, St. Charles street. Officers—W. M. Burwell, of the Republican, President; Henry S. Armstrong, of the Times, Vice President; J. E. Sliger, of the Picayune, Recording Secretary; Paul Waterman, Corresponding Secretary; Jacob Hassenger, of the German Gazette, Treasurer; John Fairfax, E. G. Dill andV. C. Dentzell, Stewards.

THE NEW ORLEANS CLUB.

Club House No. 148 Canal street. Organized May 15, 1875. Officers—Dr. B. A. Pope, President; Hon. F. A. Monroe, Vice President; J. O. Nixon, Jr., Secretary and Treasurer; P. Buchanan, D. A. S. Vaught, J. D. Huger, Governing Committee.

PICKWICK CLUB.

Club House corner of Canal street and Exchange Place. Officers: T. C. Herndon, President; Wm. M. Owen, Secretary; J. J. Stewart, Treasurer.

BOSTON CLUB.

Club House No. 4, Carondelet street. Established 1841. Chartered 1867.

Officers: Dr. Samuel Choppin, President; J. M. Witherspoon, Vice President; Wm. Bell, Secretary,

ORLEANS ROWING CLUB.

Boat House on the river, opposite the Shippers' Press. Officers: Sam Boyd, President; B. D. Wood, First Vice President; R. A. Browne, Second Vice President; Theo. J. Wells, Secretary; James R. McConnel, Treasurer; Jas.

McKeon, Captain; C. B. Penrose, Lieutenant; Nat. N. McGrath, W. H. Maning and James Kirkpatrick, on Governing Committee.

I. O. B. B.

Officers of District Grand Lodge, No. 7, for 1875: Grand President, Max Dinkelspeil, of New Orleans; First Vice President, M Selig, of Memphis; Second Vice President, M. H. Jacobi, of Montgomery, Ala.; Grand Secretary, M. Ulman, of Memphis, Tenn.; Grand Treasurer, T. Haffek, of Memphis; Sergeant-at-Arms, Charles L. Gross, of Canton, Miss.

GRAND DIVISION, SONS OF TEMPERANCE.

Meets quarterly, in January, April, July, and October. Officers: Joseph Magner, President; M. L. Navra, Vice Geo. Grindley, G. W. P.; Chas. Rosseter, Grand Scribe; H. S. Bell, Grand Treasurer.

HARMONY CLUB.

Club House Odd Fellow's Hall, Camp street. President; Selim Barnett, Treasurer; Simon Cohn, Secretary; Julius Weiss, Leopold Loeb, Fred. Gumble, executive committee; S. Miller, Manager.

PROMINENT BUSINESS HOUSES.

The high reputation for promptness and integrity enjoyed by the merchants of New Orleans may very justly be a source of pride to all classes of her citizens. Their caution, prudence and good judgment are well known; speculation seldom has a place on their books; their transactions, however immense, are real, and consequently rest upon a firm and reliable basis. As a grocery market New Orleans possesses greater advantages than any other city in the country, and in this department of her commerce many of the most reliable business men of the city are engaged. Prominent among the houses in this branch of trade is the popular firm of

FLASH, LEWIS & CO.,

whose spacious stores corner of Gravier, Peters and Fulton streets occupy a front of four numbers on the first named, and five numbers on each of the two latter streets. With ample capital, energy and rare capacity, combined with promptness, courtesy and fair dealing, they have secured a business whose ramifications extend to twenty-one States of the Union, and demands facilities and accommodations of the most improved descriptions. We may safely say that as recently refitted, their establishment is a model of its kind, and as perfect for the uses for which it has been so admirably designed as can be found anywhere. A large passage way on the ground floor extends from Peters to Fulton streets, enabling them to receive and ship goods under cover, and with the aid of tarpaulins, to be independent of the weather in the prompt transaction of their business. On the same floor are the sample rooms, the offices of the receiving, shipping and invoice departments, all arranged with a view to the speedy and convenient dispatch of the work devolving upon each. A handsome stairway leads to the stories above, where are the private offices of the members of the firm and cashier, kook-keepers, correspondent and others, and in the fitting up of all of these, comfort, elegance and refined taste have been combined. The vast building, or series of buildings, give ample room for the storage of the varied stock required by their trade, and every facility for its handling has been provided. A specialty of this house is sugar and molasses, in which they do a very large business. Having a thorough knowledge of the trade, and being constantly in the market, they are enabled to give their customers every advantage, a fact which is appreciated by merchants in Virginia, the States of the West, and in Texas, who receive their supplies from this prompt and energetic firm. Having correspondents in the leading markets of the West, they receive from first hands large shipments of pork, bacon, flour, etc., thus making a business combining the products of our own and other States, the annual total of which runs up to millions of dollars. To properly conduct this immense trade sixty employees are required, and these have been selected for their experience, energy and integrity, each person having a position suited to his capacity and skill.

No house in the country can boast of a brighter record than that of

JOHN I. ADAMS & CO.,

whose experience in the grocery trade of New Orleans extends through a period of over thirty years. Their stores, Nos. 43, 45 and 47 Peters street, present during the business hours of the day a scene of activity, life and bustle which indicates to the observer the variety and extent of their business, yet through all, order reigns supreme. Dealing largely in box and can goods, fancy groceries, whiskies, wines and liquors, which they are enabled to secure to the best advantage through their New York house, Jay L. Adams & Co., they also receive heavy consignments from the millers and packers of the West, of flour, pork, bacon, and other produce, thus enabling them to supply their wide circle of customers at the lowest market rates, while the large trade which they enjoy with all points contiguous to New Orleans enables them to place to the best advantage the goods consigned to them by their correspondents. In the house will be found many of the oldest men connected with the grocery trade of our city ; men whose faces have been familiar to, and whose promptness, energy and fair dealing have made them popular with purchasers in this market for many years past, With ample capital, long experience and a thorough knowledge of the wants of the people of this section, this old and substantial house has done and is still doing its full share towards making New Orleans the most popular market of the South-west.

One of the most popular of our wholesale grocery houses is that of

SCHMIDT & ZIEGLER,

whose extensive establishment is at Nos. 49, 51, 53 and 55 South Peters street, between Natchez and Poydras. The spacious building is filled with every article known to the trade, and a very large force of employees, all prompt, courteous and reliable, are kept constantly engaged in packing, marking and shipping the goods ordered by their many correspondents from all sections of this and neighboring States.

Messrs. Schmidt & Ziegler are agents for the States of Louisiana and Texas for the celebrated Piper Heidseik champagne, a wine which has stood the test of years and is everywhere appreciated by connoisseurs of the juice of the grape. They have also a large stock of old and pure whiskies, brandies and wines in which their trade is extensive. So admirably arranged are their stores, and their business conducted with such skill, that every thing moves like clock work throughout the whole establishment, and every year adds to the popularity of the firm

Among the favorite grocery houses of New Orleans is that of

HARTWELL & CHAMBERS,

Nos. 36 Tchoupitoulas and 34 Peters streets, who have through a long period of years enjoyed the confidence and esteem of all who know them. They carry a large line of coffee, sugar, flour. rice, tobacco, case goods and wines and liquors, which are excelled by none in our extensive market. Always prompt and courteous in their dealings, their large and constantly increasing trade is the natural result of their energy, perseverance and hônorable system of conducting busness.

KEEP, RAYMOND & CO.

This house, Nos. 77 and 79 Poydras street, is deservedly esteemed one of the staunchest and most reliable in the country. On the first of September last they admitted as a partner Mr. R. S. Rickey, formerly with Flash, Lewis & Co., and added a wholesale grocery department to their already extensive business.

The house was established over a third of a century ago, by Mr. E. S. Keep, and under various titles, but always preserving its identity, has existed ever since, commanding unlimited confidence at home and abroad. In conjunction with the Western produce commission business, in which they are so well known, they will give special attention to sugar, molasses, coffee, rice and tobacco. With ample capital, long experience and indomitable energy, they are prepared to give their correspondents the best advantages of this market.

BERCIER & DE SMET.

Among the importers of wines, liquors and French

goods, no house stands higher than that of Messrs. Bercier & DeSmet, No. 43 Decatur (Old Levee) street, agents for the South of Messrs. Otard, Dupuy & Co., Jules Robin & Co., Seignouret Freres, Javerzac Viremondry & Co., and other old and esteemed French houses. They have always in store and in bond, claret, white wines, cognac, sardines, petits pois, champignons and other choice imported goods, which they can sell at the lowest market prices.

One of the old time establishments of our city is the great hardware firm of

A. BALDWIN & CO.,

Nos. 74 Canal and 91 to 95 Common streets, successors to Slocomb, Baldwin & Co., importers of foreign hardware, cutlery, etc., and dealers in plantation implements, carpenter's tools, &c:, &c.

The house was established in 1822, and with the exception of the interruption caused by the war, has been in active operation ever since, and always characterized by liberality and fair dealing. Their handsome store is an ornament to our leading thoroughfare, and its spacious rooms, and several warehouses in other parts of the city, are kept constantly filled with every article belonging to their department of commerce, which they can sell as low as any house in America.

Another of the leading business points is the well known dry goods store of

D. H. HOLMES,

155 Canal street, and 15 Bourbon street. As a first-class emporium of the finest imported fabrics; as well as the most serviceable domestic goods, this house has a reputation of over thirty years.

It is one of the most elegantly arranged business places in our city, having a spacious building, with wide front on Canal street, which is of great depth, stocked with silks, dress goods, domestics, etc., and a connecting side store opening on Bourbon street, devoted to gloves, laces, velvet and other fine goods.

M. H. APPLEGATE.

This merchant, whose store is at No. 146 Poydras street, enjoys a well earned reputation as a plumber and dealer in cooking ranges and boilers, bath tubs, force and lifting pumps, etc.

The St. James Hotel, and many other large establishments, contain specimens of Mr. Applegate's work, which always gives the highest satisfaction.

STAUFFER, MACREADY & CO.

For nearly half a century this house has held a prominent and honored place in the trade of New Orleans. One of the characteristics of this firm is that all of its members have grown up in the house, advancing step by step, until they became proprietors in the business which their skill and energy had done so much to build up. Thus they are not only experienced in their business, but well acquainted with all the old customers of the firm. Their stores are Nos. 71 Canal and 11 to 23 Dorsier streets, extending through to Custom House street, and in them is stored an extensive stock of cutlery, iron, nails; shelf and heavy hardware, plows, etc., and their ample capital and superior facilities, enable them to offer their customers the best inducements in the market.

Prominent among the drug houses of the South stands that of

I. L. LYONS,

Successor to Ball, Lyons & Co., corner of Camp and Gravier streets. Mr. Lyons keeps an immense stock of foreign and domestic drugs, patent medicines, surgical implements, etc., and enjoys a trade which extends throughout the South-west. He is proprietor of the celebrated Garryowen Bitters, Abram's Chill Tonic, Brodies Cordial, and other preparations which have been used extensively for many years past, always giving relief to the patient and satisfaction to the physician who recommends them in his practice.

We refer with pleasure to the agency of the Piedmont & Arlington Life Insurance Company of Virginia, under the direction of that courteous and able gentleman,

MAJOR G. W. TERRELL,

whose admirable management of the affairs of the company in this section, has made it so popular with our people. Maj. Terrell is also agent for the Southern

Historical Society and Southern Educational Instutitions, and conducts the different departments of his extensive business, with so much energy and care that everything goes on with the regularlty of clock-work.

Presuming that many of our readers will want to supply themselves with clothing, we refer them to

PIERSON & HEWS,

Nos. 13 and 15 Camp street, opposite the ladies' entrance to the City Hotel. This firm keeps a large stock, from which business suits and elegrnt ball room and party suits may be selected. Their goods are neat and stylish and may be relied upon as to quality, while their prices are always reasonable. They will also make up clothing at short notice, guaranteeing a comfortable fit and the best of work.

Planters and commission merchants should bear in mind that

GAUTHREAUX & WRIGHT,

No. 56 Camp street, are agents for the Victor Standard Scales, which have been recognized as thoroughly reliable wherever used. Composed of two of our most enterprising young merchants, this firm is prepared to offer every advantage to purchasers, whether at wholesale or retail.

New Orleans is famed as a depot for the importation of French wines and fancy goods, and among those in this business none are more reliable than

PAUL GILPI & BROTHER,

No. 41 Decatur, (Old Levee,) street. They are sole agents in the South of A. C. Menkon & Co's cognac, P. Clemont & Co's M. Boutet Clarets, F. Pam's Burgundy Ports and other favorite houses, and keep a large stock of cherries and fruits in brandy, prunes, green peas, mushrooms, etc., etc. Dealers and connoisseurs will do well to give them a call.

E. W. RODD & SONS.

This firm, which has been identified with the wholesale molasses, syrups, and coffee trade of our city for over twenty years, is located at Nos. 14, 15, 16, 17, 18 and 19 North Front street, between Custom House and Bienville streets. Their long experience in the trade, ample capital and superior facilities, give them great advantages in the market, and planters and dealers will do well to effect arrangements with them for the sale of their stocks and the filling of their orders.

Among the attractions of New Orleans is the beautiful Grunewald Hall, on Baronne street near Canal, where is located the spacious piano warerooms of

LOUIS GRUNEWALD,

who keeps a large stock of pianos, organs, musical instruments, and music, which embraces all that is new artistic and desirable.

The fame of the Charter Oak Stove is so extensive and the name of

RICE BROTHERS & CO.,

the agents, Nos. 89 and 91 Camp and 597 Magazine streets, has been so intimately connectad with it, that people are apt to overlook the fact that this staunch old firm keep also an extensive stock of heavy and shelf hardware, cutlery, guns, agricultural implements, etc., which they buy from first hands and can sell as low as any house in the South. Recent improvements have made the Charter Oak as nearly perfect as human skill can approach, a fact which housekeepers should remember.

The veteran of the crockery trade,

ISIDORE LEVI,

will be found at Messrs. A. Piser & Co's. 24 Magazine street, ready to supply his friends with the finest cut and engraved glassware, (real Backrat,) decorated china, Parian figures and crockery in crates for the country trade. Direct importing enables them to sell at New York prices.

No visitor should leave the city without calling at the extensive book establishment of

R. G. EYRICH,

No. 130 Canal street, where will be found elegant stationery, the latest novels, fashion magazines, and all the polite reading of the day, as well as school, medical and miscellaneous books.

The Fairbanks' Standard Scale Company have an active and energetic agent in our well known citizen,

W. B. BOWMAN,

No. 53 Camp street, from whom our visitors can purchase as reliable goods as can be found anywhere.

LOUISIANA STEAM SASH FACTORY.

This is one of the most extensive establishments of our city, occupying from No. 299 to 307 on Gravier street. Messrs. Roberts & Co., the proprietors, are known throughout the South and West as prompt, enterprising and liberal merchaats. Their sash, blinds, doors, mouldings, balusters, etc., are not only used here, but are shipped to distant markets, the great demand keeping constantly employed a large force of skilled workmen. They manufacture school room furniture, which, for convenience, strength and beauty is superior to any we have ever seen, and we may add that all their work is finished in the most complete and thorough style.

The pioneer of the sewing machine business in New Orleans was the late Samuel H. Peck, Esq., of whom

M. A. PECK,

No. 149 Canal street, is the son and successor. He is agent for the Wheeler & Wilson Sewing Machine, the excellence of which, in every class of sewing, is every where acknowledged. Mr. Peck is an energetic, prompt and courteous gentleman, with whom it is a pleasure to do business.

Gentlemen will find at

H. B. STEVENS & CO'S

No. 135 Canal street, a new and fashionable stock of clothing, all selected with great care for their own special trade. They will make up at short notice suits of any desired material, for which they employ the most competent workmen. This firm does business on the one price principle, and have an enviable reputation for courtesy, promptness and fair dealing towards all who call on them.

One of the oldest wholesale boot and shoe establishments in the South is that of

JOHN M. GOULD,

No. 8 Magazine street. Possessing every facility for his business, and a thorough knowledge of the wants of our people, Mr. Gould is enabled to offer superior inducements to all merchants and dealers who want goods in his line.

We advise planters and all interested in improved plantation machinery to call at

NEW ORLEANS MACHINERY DEPOT,

Nos. 166 Gravier and 17 Union streets. Mr. C. B. Churchill, the manager, is an old, experienced and practical mechanic, who has spent over thirty years in constructing and selling machinery in the South, and in his recommendations the most implicit confidence may be placed. Mr. Chas. G. Johnsen, the proprietor, is also well known as a reliable merchant and machinery dealer. They have steam engines, pumps, corn and wheat mills, cotton presses, and all other kinds of plantation machinery.

A. THOMSON & CO,

This old house has recently removed to the corner of Gravier and Tcoupitoulas streets, which they have fitted up in an elegant manner and supplied with all the conviences required for their business. As purchasing commission merchants in sugar, molasses and rice, their long experience and ample capital enable them to offer the best advantages of this market to their customers.

The popular wholesale drug house of

WHEELOCK, FINLAY & CO.,

is at No. 35 Magazine street. They are proprietors of Wilhoft's Tonic, Argyle Bitters, and many other specifics which have gained a wide celebrity. The house dates from anti-bellum days, and has always stood high in the esteem of our community.

Lovers of music should call on

PHILIP WERLEIN,

Nos. 80, 82 and 90 Baronne street, at whose mammoth establishment they will find a splendid stock of new pianos from the best makers in the world. Estay organs which are every where favorites, musical instruments, and music in endless variety. He has also second-hand pianos in good order. Mr. Werlein has had a life long experience in his business, and his extended trade shows that he understands the tastes of our people and is determined to please.

Who has not heard of Muir & Son's Edinburgh Ale, Burke's Guinness Stout and Ale, and Allsopp's Ale, articles of world-wide fame, which can be obtained in the original packages from

RARESHIDE & MAES,

No. 17 Thoupitouslas street, sole agents for these celebrated goods. Messrs. Rareshide & Maes import besides, brandies, clarets, Ramsay's Scotch whiskies, olive oils, etc., etc., which they offer to the trade at the lowest market rates.

While in our city do not fail to call on

B. T. WALSHE,

No. 110 Canal street, who can supply you with gloves, cravats, and handsome imported underwear, Balbriggan hose, and good serviceable shirts, at low prices. Capt. Walshe is one of our most energetic and public spirited citizens, he is fully up to the times, and besides is a gentleman whose sterling qualities have made him a favorite with all who know him.

One of the most enterprising firms in our city is that of

S. HERNSHEIM & BROTHER,

Nos. 60, 71 and 73 Gravier street, importers and wholesale dealers in cigars, leaf and manufactured tobacco. They have an extensive trade with Texas, Mexico and Central America, and are noted for the excellence of their brands, their low prices, and liberal dealings.

Shall we say a word in favor of the

SOUTHERN PUBLISHING AND ADVERTISING HOUSE,

No. 56 Camp street, up stairs? Modesty forbids. Let those who are pleased testify their satisfaction by their continued favors.

In conclusion we desire to return thanks for appreciated favors to our old and valued friend John M. Colby, No. 20 St. Charles street, the courteous and obliging general agent for the great publishing house of D. Appleton & Co.

EDUCATIONAL.

The history of New Orleans is replete with evidences to prove that the cause of "schools for the instruction of the young," received early attention from the founders and first settlers of the city, and that, notwithstanding assertions to the contrary by persons ignorant of our institutions, the development of the mind by means of liberal education, has ever been a cherished and well supported scheme by the people of the Crescent City.

URSULINE CONVENT.

The school of the Ursuline Nuns, who arrived here in 1727, five years after the settlement of the city, was the first we find mentioned, and was in reality the first established here. For almost a century, till 1824, their labors were continued at their old convent, at the corner of Conde, now Chartres, and Ursuline streets, when they removed to their present spacious one near the Barracks, where they are still engaged in that admirable cause of which they were the pioneers in this city.

A complete history of this institution would be too lengthy for a work like the present, nor is it necessary; the Ursuline Convent has a national, indeed wider reputation, as an institution where all the accomplishments, and branches of a thorough education are imparted to girls, and all the graces of the mind and heart cultivated and fostered.

The subjoined extract shows in what light this time-honored school has ever been regarded; for the description is as applicable to its workings at the present time, as to the near or remote past, with this exception, that its influence and patronage is now more extended.

In a private letter to President Jefferson, Dec. 27, 1803, Gov. Claiborne writes: "I yesterday paid a visit of ceremony to the Ursuline Convent, and returned deeply impressed with its value and importance. There is a Lady Abbess or Superior, and eleven nuns who devote themselves to the education of girls. They, at present, accommodate seventy-three boarders, and a hundred day scholars. The children of the opulent of Louisiana, and a number from Mississippi here receive instructions, nor do they close their doors on the poor. Many are here received gratutiously and treated with the utmost kindness by these benevolent women. The society was under the Spanish dominion much larger, but many of the nuns, on the transfer of Louisiana to France, shocked by the incidents of the French revolution, sought an asylum in Havana. A number of these, I am informed, will soon return, confiding in the protection of our Government."

COLLEGE OF THE IMMACULATE CONCEPTION.

This college for boys, which is under the care of the Jesuit Fathers, Baronne, near Canal street, is another of the old time institutions of New Orleans. There are at present nearly three hundred pupils under the competent instructions and judicious care of this society, than whom none are more distinguished for learning, eloquence, and urbanity of manner.

Faculty and other College Officers: Very Rev. F. Gautrelet, S. J., President; Rev. P. Bouige, S. J., Vice President; Rev. A. Jourdan. S. J„ Rev. D. Hubert, S. J. Chaplains; Rev. D. McKiniry, S. J., Secretary; Mr. M. Kelly, S. J., Professor of Rhetoric and Belles Lettres; Mr. Ch. Klein, S. J., Professor of first and second grammar class; M. N. Davis, S. J., Professor of third grammar class; Rev. A. Jourdan, Professor first commercial class; Rev. A. Jourdan, Professor of second commercial class; Rev. T. MacElligot, S. J., Assistant Professor of second commercial class; Rev. V. Jouannet, Professor of first preparatory class; Rev. Father Gelat, S. J., Professor of second preparatory class; Mr. Perelli, Drawing Master.

ST. MARY'S DOMINICAN CONVENTS.

These schools conducted by the Nuns of St. Dominic, have acquired an enviable reputation, although but of comparitively recent establishment. At the mother house, corner of Dryades and Calliope streets, as well as at the branch house, Greenville, near Carrollton, all branches of a thorough practical education, and, except dancing, every accomplishment, music, drawing, painting, etc., are taught to the pupils. To the deaf and dumb these excellent ladies extend instructions, and the proficiency and general information of those afflicted ones, have often been the themes of compliment and admiration at the annual Commencement Exercises of these schools. Sister Mary John, sub-Prioress, Dryades street, Sister Mary Genevieve, Prioress, Greenville.

PEABODY HIGH SCHOOL.

This Young Ladies' Academy, corner St. Andrew and Coliseum, is under the supervision of Mrs. Kate Shaw, whose name has been familiar for many years, to all interested in the cause of education. As a judicious disciplinarian Mrs. Shaw ranks among the first in the country, and her flourishing school is ample evidence of her abilities as a teacher.

PEABODY NORMAL SCHOOL.

This Academy, partly supported from the Peabody educational fund, is directed by Professor Robert M. Lusher, a gentleman who has ever identified himself with the schools of our State, and whose name is sufficient guaranty that the Normal School, so as far as the means at disposal will permit, is well and ably conducted.

HEBREW EDUCATIONAL SOCIETY SCHOOL.

Ulrich Bettison, Esq., Principal, Calliope, between Prytania and St. Charles.

We had a long list of other prominent private schools prepared for publication, and an ably written article, by a well known professor, on the "Present Condition of our Public Schools," which we regret must, for want of space, be excluded from this number of the Visitor's Guide, but which we will present in our next edition.

DENECHAUD'S

NEW  NEW

RESTAURANT,

No. 8 Carondelet Street,

Near Canal, - - - - - - - - - NEW ORLEANS.

E. F. DENECHAUD

Desires to return his thanks to the many friends who have liberally patronized him during the past fifteen years, and assures them that in his new location he is prepared to furnish every

DELICACY OF THE MARKET,

With the choicest IMPORTED WINES, ALES, etc., at very reasonable prices.

Boarders by the week or month with or without lodging.

Large and airy rooms, for private and Society Dinners.

Special attention given to

Supper and Wedding Parties

At residence.

CHARITABLE INSTITUTIONS.

There is not perhaps another city in the United States that has so many benevolent institutions as New Orleans in proportion to its population. We are absolutely certain that it has not an equal on the face of the globe in charities supported by voluntary contributions. As there are nearly one hundred of these institutions, we can subjoin but a partial list.

The Poydras Female Orphan Asylum

is one of the oldest establishments of the kind in New Orleans. Endowed by Julien Poydras, it possesses revenues from improved real estate and other sources. Magazine street, near Peters Avenue. Mrs. Mary Sugden, matron.

Female Orphan Asylum.

Intersection of Camp and Prytania. Directed by the Sisters of Charity, and supported entirely by the pew rents of St. Theresa's Church and voluntary contributions. There are nearly three hundred children at present in the institution.

St. Elizabeth Asylum,

Napoleon Avenue, corner Prytania; Sister Angelica, Superioress; for girls. In this Asylum the girls are taught trades; dressmaking, etc., needle work of all kinds, washing, ironing and cooking, and are thus enabled to earn a support after leaving the Institution.

Jewish Widows and Orphans Asylum,

Jackson street, corner Chippewa; Levi Shoenberg, Superintendent. One of the best conducted and supported institutions in the city.

St. Anna's Asylum,

For indigent females, corner Prytania and St. Mary.

German Protestant Asylum,

State, between Camp and Chestnut; Felix Schunnman, Superintendent. A visit to this Asylum will afford pleasure to all who love to see evidences of health, contentment and industry.

Little Sisters of the Poor,

Laharpe, between North Prieur and North Johnson; Sister Marie Claire, Superioress. This admirable institution is devoted to the care of the helpless aged and infirm of both sexes, and is one of the most deserving asylums in our midst, having for its wards those whom

"Age and want, oh! ill-matched pair,"

have left dependant on the charities of others.

Convent of the Good Shepherd,

Bienville, near Broad; Sister Mary Rose, Superioress. This house of refuge is intended for those unfortunates who are, it would seem sometimes, alike disclaimed by heaven and earth. There are many industries practiced in the institution for the support of its inmates, and many contributions sent by the charitable, yet owing to the large numbers that are received in the house, the means at disposal are not always equal to the demand.

Protestant Episcopal Church Home for Children,

Jackson, between Chippewa and St. Thomas; Mrs. Roberta Wingfield, Directress.

Industrial School and Model Farm of Our Lady of the Holy Cross,

Refinery and Levee, near Convent; Father Robinson, Superintendent.

Asylum for Destitute Orphan Boys,

South side St. Charles, between Valmont and Dufossat, Jefferson City; George Burns, Superintendent.

Providence Asylum for Colored Female Children,

Hospital, corner North Tonti; Mrs. Barjaque, Directress.

Home for the Aged and Infirm,

Annunciation, south west corner Calliope; Mrs. Éleanor Stokes, Matron.

THE SLAUGHTER HOUSE.

About two hundred yards below the United States Barracks is situated the buildings and yards of the Crescent City Live Stock and Slaughter House Company, which are admirably arranged for the speedy and economical execution of the work for which they were constructed. The present facilities would allow of the slaughter of 1500 head of cattle daily, and as the company owns a large tract of land, these accommodations can at any time be increased to any desirable extent. The company was incorporated in 1860, but met with strenuous opposition from the butchers and dealers until March 1871, when a compromise was effected. A visit to this place will well repay strangers who come to our city.

VIEW OF NEW ORLEANS.

Our friends who wish to enjoy a fine view of the Crescent City, with the surrounding country spread out before them, as on a map drawn by the Master of all art, Nature, should ascend the tower of St. Patrick's Church, on Camp street, between Girod and Julia. Rev. Father Allen, the rector of St. Patrick's, has made every arrangement for the safety of visitors, and has placed the price of admission at twenty-five cents. All who call will be courteously received, and this is one of the sights which should not be missed.

SOUTHERN STATES AGRICULTURAL AND INDUSTRIAL EXPOSITION.

This exhibition, for which the most thorough preparation has been made, will open on the Fair Grounds in our city on the 26th of February, 1876, and continue ten days. It is designed as a thorough exposition of the agricultural and mechanical products of the Southern States, Mexico and Central America, but will be open to competition from all quarters of the country, and the inquiries for space and other information already received, justifies the anticipation that it will be one of the most complete exhibitions of the kind ever held in the Union.

The premium list has been carefully prepared, and includes liberal rewards in every branch of industry, to be awarded by competent and disinterested jurors.

The time selected for this enterprise is most opportune; February is one of the most delightful and healthy months of the year; Mardi Gras occurs on the 29th of that month, and we may safely predict that at that time our city will be full of strangers. Favorable arrangements have been secured for the transportation of goods and visitors from every section.

The Executive Committee is composed of gentlemen well known for their energy and integrity, and the General Superintendent, Mr. Samuel Mullen, is a good organizer and persistent worker, who has given all his time and energies to the project. Full information may be obtained by addressing Mr. Mullen, and prompt and courteous replies may be relied upon to all inquiries.

PLEASURE EXCURSIONS.

The environs of New Orleans afford many agreeable retreats, a visit to any one of which will well repay the pleasure seeker.

CARROLLTON GARDENS.

The trip to Carrollton is deservedly one of the most popular excursions in the neighborhood of our city. The green cars from the corner of Canal and Baronne street, only a short distance from the principal hotels and boarding houses, take passengers through one of the pleasantest avenues, lined by palatial residences and smiling gardens, to that suburban district of New Orleans. Here are situated the Carrollton Gardens, which for many years have been a favorite resort with our people. and a place much admired by strangers. These gardens have recently been purchased by Mr. C. F. Conrad, who has spared neither trouble or expense to improve them. The spacious walks are lined with the choicest flowers, whose beautiful bloom and gentle fragrance are especially attractive to those who come from the North, where snow and ice greet the eye on every hand. Instead of snow balls the visitor may obtain an exquisitely arranged boquet or the rarest of plants, and in place of sleet and ice, he will see a verdure most pleasing to the senses. Connected with the gardens there is a spacious building, with large, airy and comfortable rooms, which Mr. Conrad will keep as a private family hotel, on the European plan, with a restaurant, where the most inviting meals, with all the substantials and delicacies afforded by our markets may be obtained, and at reasonable prices. Mr. Conrad is now erecting bath houses, where sulphur, and warm or cold baths may be obtained. He will also give weekly concerts in his gardens, having made arrangements with one of the most popular and successful musical directors for that purpose.

Dinner parties, weddings, etc., will be accommodated in the best of style, and the gardens may be rented, on application to Mr. C. F. Conrad, for private parties, pic-nics, etc.

No visitor to our city should fail to go to the

HALF WAY HOUSE.

Situated just over the bridge, at the intersection of Canal street and the new canal, and accessible by the Canal street cars, fare five cents each way. The house is kept in first class style, and refreshments of the best kind may be had at moderate prices. The garden is about five hundred feet front by four hundred in depth, and is under the highest state of cultivation, having been tended with care for the past thirty-five years. Here seats and arbours are arranged along the well kept walks, making a delightful retreat for visitors. The nursery is very extensive and contains all the rare fruit and ornamental trees, shrubs, flowers and plants known to our climate, which may be purchased of the proprietor, Mr. S. Fasnacht, who resides on the place, who will also supply boquets to those wanting them.

These gardens have always been a favorite resort for families and pleasure seekers. A fine dancing platform, expressly for private parties, was erected last spring and now every convenience for pic-nics and private parties will be found on the grounds, which may be rented for these purposes. In the near neighborhood will be seen the Metaire, Greenwood and other beautiful cemeteries.

AN EXCURSION ON THE LAKE.

Having enjoyed some of the drives in and around New Orleans and visited a few of the popular resorts, we will now take an excursion on the lake, confident that it will not be the least pleasant of our trips in the Crescent City. Taking the Ponchartrain railway, we will proceed to the Lake End and board the popular steamer Camelia, commanded by that courteous gentleman and thorough officer, Capt. Hanover. Leaving the wharf we steam out into the lake, enjoying the salt sea breeze, and the calm, rest inspiring atmosphere. Although we have already breakfasted, in less than an hour we are as hungry as a soldier after a day's march, and hail with delight the clang of the bell which says that the morning meal is ready. Proceeding to the saloon we see a table loaded with the most tempting eatables, and at once "falling to," we are surprised no less at the heartiness of our appetite, than at the reasonable price exacted for our indulgence. After a pleasant sail of about three hours the picturesque village of Mandeville is approached. This is a favorite summer resort with many of our oldest creole families, and is famed for its excellent fishing and bathing accommodations. From this point we proceed to Lewisburg and Madisonville, both pleasant villages, and on the return trip of the boat come back to the city.

Mr. Cohen M, Soria, No. 18 Union street, is agent for the Camelia, and from him all information in relation to this trip may be obtained.

UNITED STATES BARRACKS.

A trip to the Barracks is considered one of the pleasantest excursions in the neighborhood of New Orleans. The distance from Canal street is about three and three-quarter miles, and the whole distance may be accomplished by the street cars at an expense of five cents each way. The buildings used by the French Government and afterwards by the Federal authorities as a barracks, were located on Chartres street just below the present residence of Archbishop Perche. The present site was well chosen and the arrangements of the place are perfect and complete.

MILNEBURG,

or, as it is more popularly known, the "Old Lake End," is the terminus of the Pontchartrain railroad. It is directly on the banks of the old lake, and the cool air always prevailing, the sails, fishing and bathing to be enjoyed, make it a favorite resort with all who wish to enjoy a day away from the brick and mortar of the Crescent City.

MAGNOLIA GARDENS,

situated on the Bayou St. John in close proximity to the boat houses of the Pelican and St. John Rowing Clubs, is a pleasant resort. The garden is a favorite place of entertainment with our citizens, particularly with those of German birth or extraction, as the place is conducted on the German plan. Here is located the park of the

NEW ORLENS RIFLE CLUB,

an old and favorite organization devoted to the now national pastime of rifle shooting, numbering among its members many of the leading gentlemen of our city. All who may feel disposed to visit their park may rest assured of a courteous and kind reception.

IMPORTANT POINTS.

SOUTHERN EXPRESS COMPANY—164 Gravier and 15 Union, between St. Charles and Carondelet Streets.

WESTERN UNION TELEGRAPH COMPANY—Corner Gravier and St. Charles streets.

BALIZE TELEGRAPH COMPANY—35½ Carondelet street.

STOKER'S EUROPEAN TELEGRAPH AGENCY—22 Union street.

POST OFFICE—In Custom House, Decatur street, bet. Canal and Customhouse streets.

NEW ORLEANS CHAMBER OF COMMERCE—120 Common street.

NEW ORLEANS COTTON EXCHANGE—187 Gravier street.

MECHANICS' INSTITUTE—Dryades, between Canal and Common streets.

MERCHANTS' EXHCANGE—Provisions and Western produce—corner Tchoupitoulas and Poydras streets.

NEW ORLEANS SCHOOL OF MEDICINE—Corner Common and Villere streets.

UNIVERSITY BUILDINGS—Corner Common and Baronne streets.

CITY GOVERNMENT.

CHARLES J. LEEDS............................Mayor.
EDWARD PILSBURY.......Administrator of Finance.
JAMES G. BROWN.........Administrator of Accounts.
P.L. BOUNY............Administrator of Assessments.
E. A. BURKE..........Administrator of Improvements.
LEON BERTOLI.....Adm'r of W. W. & Pub. Buildings.
J. O. LANDRY...........Administrator of Commerce.
DENNIS McCARTHY.........Administrator of Police.
B. F. JONAS..........................City Attorney.
T. S. HARDEE.........................City Surveyor.
GUSTAVE Le GARDEUR..................City Notary.

COURTS.

Supreme Court—Court House, Chartres street, opposite Jackson Square—Hon. John T. Ludeling, Chief Justice; Hons. James G. Taliaferro, Rufus K. Howell, P. Hickey Morgan and W. G. Wyly, Associate Justices; John M. Howell, Clerk. First Judicial District embraces the parish and city of New Orleans.

Superior Court—Jacob Hawkins, Judge; John Burke, Clerk.

Superior Criminal Court—Hiram R. Steele, Judge; John Fitzpatrick, Clerk.

DISTRICT COURTS.

First District—Edmund Abell, Judge; John R. Clay, Clerk.

SECOND DISTRICT—A. L. Tissot, Judge; Frank Pace, Jr., Clerk.

THIRD DISTRICT—Edmund Meunier, Judge; C. A. Baque, Clerk.

FOURTH DISTRICT—B. L. Lynch, Judge; Edward De Blois, Clerk.

FIFTH DISTRICT—E. N. Cullom, Jndge; Thomas Duffy, Clerk.

SIXTH DISTRICT—Arthur Saucier, Judge; John J. O'Brien, Clerk.

—o—

MUNICIPAL COURTS.

FIRST—Office, Davidson's Row, Carondelet, between Poydras and Lafayette streets; W. L. Evans, Judge.

SECOND—Office, second floor Criminal Court building Eugene Staes, Judge.

THIRD—Office, 87 Elysian Fields street, Webster Long, Judge.

FOURTH—Office, Rousseau street, near Jackson; Lucien Adams, Judge.

FIFTH—Office, Carrollton Avenue, between Hampson and Second streets; A. G. Brice, Judge.

ATTORNEYS AT LAW.

BUCK & DINKELSPIEL,
27 Commercial Place.

MCENERY, ELLIS & ELLIS,
No. 56 Camp street.

JOSEPH A. QUINTERO, (Consul for Costa Rica)
No. 66 Camp street.

JAMES LINGAN,
No. 122 Gravier street.

GEO. H. BRAUGHN,
17 Commercial Place.

C. MCRAE SELPH,
No. 6 Carondelet street.

W. B. LANCASTER,
No. 122 Gravier street.

JOHN J. FINNEY,
No. 13 Commercial Place.

RICE & WHITAKER,
No. 13 Commercial Place.

J. Q. A. FELLOWS,
13 Commercial Place.

LEOVY & MONROE,
28 Natchez street, Morgan Building.

E. W. HUNTINGTON,
No. 11 Exchange Place.

JOHN J. BARNETT,
No. 9 Carondelet street.

NOTARIES.

WM. B. SEYMOUR,
Notary Public and Commissioner of Deeds, for Texas, Illinois, Mississippi, and other States—Passports procured from the State Department in Washington.
79 Customhouse street.

A. Hero, Jr.,
U.S. Commissioner and Notary Public,
17 Commercial Place.

Marcel T. Ducros,
Notary Public and Commissioner of Deeds,
Room 9, No. 18 Royal street, up stairs,

Abel Dreyfous,
Notary Public,
48 Exchange Place.

James Fahey,
U. S. Commissioner and Notary Public,
158 Common street.

John J. Barnett,
Notary Public,
9 Carondelet street.

Joseph A. Quintero, Consul for Costa Rica,
Notary Public,
66 Camp street.

FERRIES.

First District—New Orleans and Algiers—Ferry landing, Canal street.

Second District—New Orleans and Algiers—Ferry landing, St. Ann street.

Third District—New Orleans and Algiers—Ferry landing, Elysian Fields street.

Fourth District—New Orleans and Gretna—Ferry landing, Jackson street.

Morgan's La. and Texas R. R. Ferry—From the foot of St. Ann street to railroad depot, Algiers.

Slaughter House Company's Ferry—From and to the Slaughter House, Algiers.

LOUISIANA AVENUE FERRY—To Harvey's Canal—Starts from foot of Louisiana Avenue.

UPPER LINE FERRY—From the foot of Upper Line to Gretna.

CLAY STATUE.

Owing to its central location and its artistic merits, this is one of the most familiar sights of New Orleans. Canal street is the great artery of the city, through which the crowds of business men, pleasure seekers and fashionable promenaders circulate and Clay Statue, standing in the most prominent part of this popular avenue, is naturally a point of interest and rendezvous.

The statue was inaugurated on the 12th of April, 1856, during the administration of Gerard Stith as mayor of our city. Col. J. B. Walton, the veteran commander of the celebrated battalion of Washington Artillery, was Grand Marshal on the occasion, and Col. J. O. Nixon First Assistant Marshal. The artist, Joel T. Hart, of Kentucky, was present; Wm. H. Hunt, Esq., was orator of the day, and J. Q. A. Fellows, Esq., was Grand Master, and led the Masonic bodies. The inauguration occasioned one of the largest and most enthusiastic public gatherings ever witnessed in our city. It was at the base of this statue that the people met on the now historic "Fourteenth of September," 1874, and called upon the usurpers to surrender the places and power they had so long held by force. Like the "Tea Party" of Boston, this action struck a sympathetic chord in the hearts of freemen everywhere, and made the Clay Statue of New Orleans a point of interest throughout the civilized world.

MARKETS.

The markets of New Orleans form a distinctive feature in its customs, and the stranger who fails to visit them during hours of sale, misses a variety in trading that cannot be found elsewhere.

FRENCH MARKET.

This, the pioneer of public markets in New Orleans, was located during the Spanish supremacy. The first building, on the site of the meat market, was destroyed by the hurricane of 1812. The present one was built in the following year, according to the designs of J. Piernas, City Surveyor, at a cost of about $30,000.

The French Market, taken as a unity, is of an irregular ground plan, having been constructed at different periods, and may be described in general terms, as a very plain specimen of the Roman Doric order, supported by brick pillars, plastered, and covered with a slate roof.

There are three distinct and separate market places comprised in this one mart, the Meat Market, the Vegetable market, and between these, the Bazaar market. The first is what its name implies, a place where meats are exposed for sale. In the second vegitables of all kinds, fish, game, fruit and flowers, have each their seperate departments, and in the Bazaar, or middle market, every possible article in the dry goods line may be procured. Each market is separated from the other by a street, and these spaces are, during market hours, literally covered with stands on which every conceivable nicnac is offered for sale. Then such a confusion of tongues, French, Italian, Spanish, Dutch, German, and scores of other foreign marchands extolling, each in his native patois, the quality and cheapness of his article of trade, or, perhaps in disgust at your ignorance of foreign dialects, trying to tell you of the merits of their wares in English that bids utter defiance to etymology.

To see the French Market in its glory one must go there on a Sunday morning between five and ten o'clock, and, if at all sensitive, put his corns in the best order, and his temper ditto, then there is no fear. An hour spent in this modern Babel will furnish the visitor, particularly if he be a stranger, with odd sounds and scenes enough to furnish subjects for speculation and amusement, for many a day at least. By all means visit the French Market.

POYDRAS MARKET.

This smaller and second edition of the old time markets, was built in 1837 on ground ceded by the Carrollton Railroad Company, "for the accommodation of the inhabitants in the rear of the second municipality." Now buildings extend for miles in the *rear* of the market, while in its immediate neighborhood are some of the best business locations in the city.

SECOND STREET MARKET.

The rapid growth of the Fourth District and its extension towards the lake, made necessary a public market in that part of town above Jackson and back of St. Charles streets. This want had long been felt, and we believe one unsuccessful attempt was made to supply it, but it remained for the energy and perseverence of a citizen of the immediate neighborhood to erect a building suitable to the wants of the people, and in its proportions be an ornament to that district.

Mr. Joseph Raymond, at the time a well known commission merchant in wool, hides, etc., took the matter in hand and the result as seen to-day reflects credit upon his rare foresight and good judgment.

The market is built on the corner of Dryades and Second streets, in the squares bounded by those two streets First and Baronne streets, in the cottage style of architecture. Graceful columns support the roof which is surmounted by a cupolo, presenting a very handsome appearance. The market is paved with the best square stone, and divided into one hundred and twenty-two roomy and well arranged stalls, where the choicest meats, fish and vegetables in their seasons may always be obtained. The market is justly popular with a wide district of our city ; those who have stalls there prepare for first class trade, by supplying the best articles at reasonable prices. The neighborhood around the Second Street Market has become one of the most flourishing in our city, large and well stocked stores where every description of goods may be obtained, have been opened and all are doing a thriving business. New and attractive residences have been built; a church and school have been established, and thus, what was a thinly settled section has become a lively thoroughfare and the property in the vicinity doubled and trebled in value.

This change is mainly due to the progressive spirit and energy of Mr. Raymond, who, appreciating the wants of the people, had the nerve to undertake and successfully carry through this great improvement. Every day additions are made, and we have no doubt that the near future will see as busy and thriving a people around the Second Street Market, as in any section of the Crescent City. Both the green and white cars, from the corner of Canal and St. Charles street pass the market, the green cars on Baronne, corner Canal, passes within one square.

ST. MARY'S MARKET.

This market, "the first section of which was constructed in 1822, by Mitchell & Lemoine," derived its name from the fact of having been built for the convenience of the residents of the "Suburb St. Mary," and was, for quite a number of years after its erection, considered very far up town. It is a very extensive building, but owing to the rapid spreading of the city in the up river direction, and the consequent removal of families, not over two-thirds of the space is now occupied ; newer and more central markets taking the lead, among these the

MAGAZINE STREET MARKET,

situated between St. Mary and St. Andrew streets, on Magazine and Old Camp streets, is one of the best supplied and patronized.

KELLER MARKET.

This building, the result of the private enterprise of the gentleman whose name it bears, is situated in the rear of

the upper part of the Fourth District, between Felicity and St. Andrew, Locust and Magnolia streets, and is a great convenience to the residents of that locality.

WASHINGTON AVENUE MARKET.

This recently constructed building is admirably arranged for the purposes of a public market. The people of the neighborhood had long felt the necessity of such an institution, and at their urgent solicitation the city authorities advertised for bids, but the only man who had sufficient confidence in the success of the enterprise to undertake its execution was Mr. Joseph Raymond, who had already built and put in operation the Second Street Market.

As soon as the contract for the Washington Avenue Market was awarded to him, Mr. Raymond proceeded energetically to put his plans in execution, and the result was the fine building where to-day all is life and activity.

The writer was present at the sale of stalls, and witnessed the lively competition between the butchers, vegetable dealers and others for stands, of which there are ninety-six. Since its construction, real estate in that vicinity has enhanced in value, and many fine residences have been erected and stores commenced. The market is conveniently located to one of our city railroad lines, and is destined to be surrounded by one of the most prosperous neighborhoods of our city. Mr. Raymond deserves great credit for his energy and perseverance in these public improvements, which have added so much to the comfort and convenience of our people. The market was opened for business on the 1st of May, 1875.

The other important public markets are

NINTH STREET MARKET.

Magazine, between Ninth and Harmony.

CLAIBORNE MARKET.

Claiborne, between Gasquet and Common.

CARROLLTON MARKET.

Dublin, corner Second, Seventh District.

NEW ORLEANS CLEARING HOUSE.

This institution was organized for business June 1st, 1872, and although the project was not at first received with favor, its admirable workings have demonstrated its usefulness, and at present, every banking institution in the city, save one, belongs to it.

Previously, the exchanges were made by the banks individually, the messengers going from bank to bank, thus consuming much valuable time, besides running risks of loss from delay and other causes. The clearings amount daily to about one and a half millions of dollars, while the balances are less than two hundred thousand dollars. By the aid of the Clearing House, the exchanges are all completed before ten o'clock, and each bank knows exactly where it stands at the commencement of the day's business.

Mr. Isaac N. Maynard is the manager of the Clearing House, and was its original projector. He is an old and highly esteemed citizen, and combines in a high degree the sterling qualities necessary in so responsible a position. The officers of the Clearing House are: President, John G. Gaines; Vice President, Samuel H. Kennedy; Manager, Isaac N. Maynard; Committee of Management, Joseph H. Oglesby, Louis Schneider and George Jonas.

BANKS.

New Orleans National Bank,

54 Camp street. A. Baldwin, President ; J. K. Bell, Vice President ; Wm. Palfrey, Cashier. Board of Directors : A. Baldwin, J. K. Bell, J. T. Burdeau, J. P. Garvey, A. Chapsky, Chas. Pleasants, Chas. Chaffe, Geo. Martin, Samuel Delgado, D. C. McCan, S. Katz, Archie Woods.

Citizens' Bank,

Corner Royal and Customhouse streets. Capital, $1,-500,000. John G. Gaines, President ; James J. Tarleton, Cashier. Directors : E. L. Carriere, John G. Gaines, Thomas D. Miller, D. A. Chaffraix, Robert Hare, J. J. Irby, Henry Renshaw.

Correspondents : Bank of America, A. D. Selleck, New York , London Joint Stock Bank ; Baring Bros. & Co., London ; Marcaurd Andre & Co.; A. & M. Heine, Paris.

Louisiana National Bank,

120 and 122 Common street. Capital, $1,000,000 ; surplus, $200,000. Jos. H. Oglesby, President ; A. Luria, Cashier Directors : J. F. D. Lanier, Thos. L. Airey, Richard Pritchard, Theo. Hellman, Henry C. Miller, W. J. Frierson, J. H. Oglesby.

Germania National Bank,

102 Canal street. Capital, $300,000; surplus, $44,000. Louis Schneider, President ; Jules Cassard, Vice President ; Henry Roehl, Cashier. Directors: Louis Schneider, Jules Cassard, Henry Abraham, J. W. Buhrmann, L. B. Cain, H. R. Gogreve, John F. Kranz, T. Prudhomme, I. K. Small.

Mutual National Bank of New Orleans,

106 Canal street Capital, $300,000 ; surplus, $184,000-

John T. Hardie, President; A. W. Bosworth, Vice President; Joseph Mitchel, Cashier. Directors: John T. Hardie, P. Maspero, P. Fourchy, J. C. VanWickle, A. Meyer, E. S. Keep, Adolph Meyer, Chas. L. Chase, L R. Coleman.

Offering days, Mondays and Thursdays; discount days, Tuesdays and Fridays.

State National Bank,

Formerly Louisiana State Bank,

33 Camp street. Capital $850,000; surplus, $38 000. Samuel H. Kennedy, President; C. L C. Dupuy, Cashier. Directors: Samuel H. Kennedy, Samuel H. Boyd, Alfred Moulton, Joseph Dunbar, Samuel Friedlander, W. G. Vincent, W. T. Blakemore, Julius Vairin.

Union National Bank,

No. 3 Carondelet street. Capital $500,000. Carl Kohn, President; James Chalaron, Cashier. Directors: A. J Gomile, W. S. Bailey, W. J. Behan, Samuel H. Snowden, Wm. Hartwell, Jos. Bowling, N. D. Wallace, W. B. Krumbhaar. B. M. Pond, E. F. Lavillebeuvre, Victor Meyer, M. M. Simpson, Carl Kohn.

Bank of Lafayette,

No. 28 Camp street. Capital $100,000. S. Hopkins, Jr., President; James Strawbridge, Cashier. Directors: J. A. Braselman, Gus. A. Breaux, Wm. G. Coyle, S. Hopkins, Jr., Geo. Johnston, Berry Russell, G. J. Fredrichs.

New Orleans Saving Institution.

No. 156 Canal street. Officers: D. Urquhart, President; Thos. A. Adams, First Vice President; Thomas A. Clarke Second Vice President; Chas. J. Leeds, Third Vice President: Charles Kilshaw, Treasurer. Trustees: Geo. Jonas, Thomas A. Adams. Thomas Allen Clarke, Chas. J. Leeds, Jules Tuyes, David Urquhart, John G. Gaines, Carl Kohn, Christian Schneider, Samuel Jamison.

Bank of America, corner Canal street and Exchange Place.

Citizens' Savings Bank, 22 Baronne street.

Hibernia National Bank, 47 Camp street.

Louisiana Savings Bank and Safe Deposit Co., 51 Camp street.

Mechanics' and Traders' Bank, 28 Carondelet street.

New Orleans and Canal Banking Co., corner Camp and Gravier streets.

St. Patrick's Hall Savings Bank, 37 Camp street.

Southern Bank, 11 St. Charles street.

Workingmen's Bank, 94 and 96 Canal street.

NEW ORLEANS BOARD OF UNDERWRITERS.

THOS. A. ADAMS, President; M. MUSSON, Vice Pres.; GEORGE MATHER, Secretary.

Office, in Louisiana National Bank Building, Nos. 120 and 122 Common streets.

INSURANCE COMPANIES.

Factors' and Traders' Insurance Company.

37 Carondelet street.

Assets, April 30, 1875..................$1,486,215 88.

Fire, River, and Marine Risks.

Ed. A. Palfrey, President; Moses Greenwood Vice President; Thos. F Walker, Secretary.

New Orleans Insurance Association.

No. 102 Canal street.

Assets, December 31, 1874 ....$494,438 79.

Fire, Marine, and River Risks.

M. Musson, President ; G. Lanaux, Secretary.

Mechanics' and Traders' Insurance Company.

14 Carondelet street.

Capital...$500,000.

Solicits Fire, River, and Marine Risks.

Lloyd R. Coleman, President ; James A. White, Secretary ; George H. Frost, Assistant Secretary and Fire Clerk ; F. C. Gregory, Marine and River Clerk ; J. Y. B. Haskell, Collector ; F. Auzout, Inspector.

Crescent Mutual Insurance Company.

67 and 69 Camp street.

Fire, Marine, and River Insurance.

Incorporated, A. D. 1849—The Oldest Mutual Insurance Company in the South.

Thomas A. Adams, President; Samuel B. Newman, Vice President; Henry V. Ogden, Secretary.

Hibernia Insurance Company.

No. 37 Camp street.

Capital...$500,000.

Insures Fire, River, and Marine Risks.

John Henderson, President ; P. Irwin, Vice President; Thomas F. Bragg, Secretary.

Sun Mutual Insurance Company.

Cash Capital.......................................$500,000.

Incorporated, January 1, 1856—With Cash Dividends to Insurers.

Issues Policies on Fire, River, and Marine Risks.

Office — Corner Camp Street and Commercial Alley.

James I. Day, President ; John G. Gaines, Vice President ; H. Carpenter, Secretary.

COMMERCIAL INSURANCE Co. of N. O.—120 Common st.

GERMANIA INSURANCE Co.—124 Common street.

HOME MUTUAL INSURANCE Co.—78 Camp street.

HOPE INSURANCE Co. of N. O.—125 Common street.

LAFAYETTE FIRE INSURANCE Co.—594 Magazine st.

MERCHANTS' MUTUAL INSURANCE Co.—104 Canal st.; branch, 77 Elysian Fields.

NEW ORLEANS INSURANCE Co.—Canal, south-east corner Camp.

PEOPLES' INSURANCE Co. of N. O.—5 St. Peter st.

TEUTONIA INSURANCE Co.—35 Camp street.

UNION INSURANCE Co.—3 Carondelet street.

NEW ORLEANS CHAMBER OF COMMERCE.

This institution, which has proved of vast importance to the business interests of our city, was organized in February, 1850. It has, like all of our institutions, had its fluctuations in fortune, but is now in a well organized and flourishing condition. Composed of a large number of our leading merchants and business men, its advocacy of our railroad interests, its pressure of good measures of legislation, and other wise acts, have resulted in great benefit to our city and State. The rooms are in the Louisiana National Bank building, Nos. 120 and 122 Common street, and the present officers are: Cyrus Bussey, President; W. C. Raymond, First Vice President; Joseph Bowling, Second Vice President; W. M. Burwell, Secretary and Treasurer.

Committee on Arbitration—R. S. Howard, A. Thomson; A. B. Griswold, A. H. Isaacson, A. Baldwin, Wm. Hartwell and E. K. Converse.

Committee on Appeals — S. H. Kennedy, W. B. Schmidt, Robert Moore, G. A Fosdick and Emory Clapp,

Executive Committee—H. O. Seixas, John Chaffe, Joseph McElroy, Louis Scherck and Johnston Armstrong.

Committee on River Obstructions—L. H. Higby, Alfred Moulton, A. K. Miller, C. G. Forshey and E. A. Yorke.

Committee on Railroads—G. W. R. Bayley, W. C. Black, W. W. Howe, C. Bussey and L. H. Joseph.

MERCHANT'S EXCHANGE.

The subject of an exchange which should combine the ability and influence of our grocery and Western produce merchants, and those following pursuits of kindred interests, had long occupied the minds of some of our leading men in those branches of commerce. On the 3d of July, 1874, a preliminary meeting was held at which Messrs. F. J. Odendahl, W. C. Raymond, B. F. Glover, R. S. Howard, J. Schwabacher, William H. Deeves, A. Hirsch, George E. Sears and H. O. Seixas, were present. It was then determined to canvass the subject and ascertain the views of those interested. So favorable was the result that in a short time sufficient funds were secured and a position selected, corner of Tchoupitoulas and Poydras streets.

The board of officers is composed of the President, five Vice Presidents and the Treasurer. The following gentlemen were selected to fill these positions: W. C. Raymond, President; R. S. Howard, Wm. Gordon, George Sears, F. J. Odendahl and E. K. Converse, Vice Presidents, and William H. Deeves, Treasurer.

As Secretary and Superintendent Mr. Samuel Mullen was selected. This gentleman performed his arduous duties in the most prompt and satisfactory manner, working with energy and perserverance to secure the success of the enterprise. Mr. Mullen continued in the

PIEDMONT AND ARLINGTON
Life Insurance Company,
OF VIRGINIA.

ASSETS $3,500,000
ANNUAL INCOME....................... 1,600,000
POLICIES ISSUED, over................ 25,000

This is the largest Southern Company in existence. Its success is beyond all precedent. It issues policies on all plans. Policies non-forfeitable. No restriction on residence or travel: All claims settled promptly. Terms very liberal.

This "Great Old Virginia Company" is doing business all over the United States and in Europe. It is the only Southern Company that has passed inspection by the Insurance Departments of New York and other States, thus placing it on the same footing of solvency with the best companies of America. It is a Home Company everywhere, because it invests its capital in every State in which it does business. Its mortality is very light—only one loss during the entire Shreveport epidemic.

Cotton Factors, Banks and Commission Merchants should insure their accounts and patrons in this company.

Remember that by insuring your lives or accounts in this excellent and reliable company you are building up a Home Institution, instead of sending your money North.

Remember that this company is located in Richmond, Va., the most prosperous and flourishing city of the South.

Remember that the officers of this company are the best financiers, most highly esteemed, successful and reliable business men in Old Virginia.

Remember that this company conducts its business at a smaller ratio of expense to income than any other company in America of its age.

Remember that the rates of this company are from $10 to $15 lower for every $1000 insurance than most other companies, they having recently raised their rates in the South.

For further particulars, address the undersigned at New Orleans, La.

Office, 28 Carondelet Street, G. W. TERRELL,
Gen. Agent and Manager, successor to Gen. D. H. Maury.

[*From the Shreveport Times.*]

In further proof of the character of the company we invite attention to the following letter from Gen. Beauregard:

OFFICE N. O. AND CARROLLTON RAILROAD CO.,
NEW ORLEANS, June 14, 1874.

To my friends in Shreveport, introducing Col. G. W. Terrell, of New Orleans, La.:

DEAR SIRS—The bearer, Col. G. W. Terrell, is the able and reliable agent of the Piedmont and Arlington Life Insurance Company, of Rich-

[SEE NEXT PAGE.]

[FROM PAGE 73.]

mond, Va. He visits your city on business connected with this Institution, which is the most liberal and prosperous of the kind in the United States. Any attention shown to Col. T. would be very acceptable to him and would much oblige,

Yours, very truly, G. T. BEAUREGARD.

Col. Terrell also brought warm letters from Gen. H. T Hays, Messrs. Pike, Brother & Co., Am. Fortier, President of the Bank of America, and many others from the most influential citizens and banks of New Orleans, all of whom indorse the Peidmont and Arlington as one of the most liberal and reliable companies in the United States.

Extract from a letter recently written by Col. W. C. Carrington, President Piedmont and Arlington Life Insurance Company of Virginia, to Col. G. W. Terrell, General Agent and Manager in New Orleans, which reads as follows, viz:

"Your past success is the highest guarantee of your fitness and ability to add additional honors to your record as a Life Agent. * * * There is no construction of proper, legal or moral duty as an Agent, or as an honest, faithful gentleman, to which you have not fully reached in all our dealings with you.

"If your record is as pure and bright in the Eternal World as in our office, you need have no dread of the future. * * * * *

"Very truly, W. C. CARRINGTON, President.

"N. B.—When it is remembered that Col. Terrell has been in the constant and active services of this excellent Virginia Company for quite six years, the above extract is very highly complimentary, and should be truly gratifying to him."

GALVESTON, Texas, May 28, 1875.

COL. G. W. TERRELL, General Agent Piedmont and Arlington Life Insurance Company, New Orleans:

Dear Sir—I enclose you my check for the amount of seventh premium of policy No. 3486, deducting the dividend. It gratifies me to see the substantial progress of our Home Company.

Very respectfully, BRAXTON BRAGG.

[SEE NEXT PAGE.]

[FROM PAGE 74.]

Orders for Bagging, Ties and goods and supplies of every description filled at the lowest market prices for cash.

Consignments of every description solicited.

Prompt and courteous attention given to all business intrusted to our care.

A NEW COMMISSION HOUSE.—We take great pleasure in directing the attention of our numerous readers to the card of our friend Col. G. W. Terrell, Cotton Factor and Commission Merchant, New Orleans, and in recommending him to the confidence and patronage of the merchants and planters of Mississippi. He is a gentleman of unimpeachable honor and integrity and of splendid business qualifications, and has secured the services of reliable gentlemen of thirty years' experience in the cotton business to assist him. He will make liberal advances on consignments, and will give prompt attention to filling orders for goods and supplies.

Col. Terrell is the General Agent in Louisiana and Mississippi for the justly popular Piedmont and Arlington Life Insurance Company, one of the very best companies in the United States.

M'me Rosa Reynoir,

MILLINERY.

The cheapest and most

FASHIONABLE MILLINERY GOODS,

In the city.

BERLIN AND ZEPHYR WORSTEDS

In all colors.

WORSTEDS.

No. 9[illegible] Chartres Street, near Canal.

WM. H. SEYMOUR,

Notary Public and Commissioner of Deeds,

For Texas, Illinois, Mississippi and other States.

PASSPORTS PROCURED from the State Department at Washington.

79 Customhouse Street,

NEW ORLEANS.

PELICAN

STEAM

Book and Job Printing

ESTABLISHMENT,

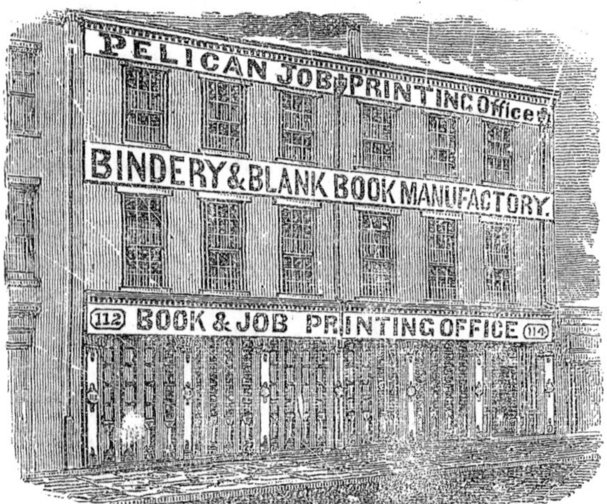

112 & 114 Poydras Street,

NEW ORLEANS, LA.

Bill Heads, Letter Heads, Note Heads, Account Sales, Notes, Drafts, Receipts, Checks, Circulars, Briefs. Cards and Printing in all its Branches

Executed with Cheapness and Dispatch.

discharge of this responsible position until a few months since, when he was selected as the General Superitendent of the Southern States Agricultural and Industrial Exposition, which will hold its first exhibition in February next.

Mr. H. S. Marks was elected to fill the vacancy occasioned by the retirement of Mr. Mullen. The Exchange is now in a flourishing condition, and is very popular with those whose business is embraced in the lines which the exchange is expected to especially benefit.

LOUISIANA RICE EXCHANGE.

Among the great products, rice must now be ranked. The extent and importance of the crop has increased yearly and approaches nearer to our other crops, sugar, molasses and cotton.

It is but a few years since little was known of Louisiana rice; it was grown from inferior seed and its culture confined to a narrow belt of country below the city. Improved seed having been introduced and attention given to its cultivation, the yield has increased both in quality and quantity, until its bulk was deemed so large by those who handled it here, as to justify the organization of a Rice Exchange. This was done a short time ago, and we have no doubt that, through this organization, a fresh impetus will be given to the planting of this grain.

The officers of the Exchange are; A. Socola, President; F. Roder, Vice President; J. David, Treasurer, and N. A. Llambias, Secretary. The Exchange room is at No. 46 Decatur street.

In our city extensive mills have been built, one of the largest being the

BROOK RICE MILL.

Nos. 89 to 93 Tchoupitoulas street, of which that most active and perservering merchant, Mr. Columbus H. Allen is proprietor. The Brook Mill is supplied with the most approved machinery for cleaning, and every facility for the expeditious receiving and handling of the grain. The quality of rice turned from this mill is unsurpassed. Mr. Allen will furnish sacks to shippers. Applications should be addressed C. H. Allen, lock box 76, New Orleans.

NEW ORLEANS STOCK EXCHANGE.

This institution organized for the better transaction of business in stocks and securities, is situated in Varieties Place, between Common and Gravier streets. The Exchange was instituted on the 4th of October last, under rules and regulations governing institutions of the same kind in New York, Boston and other large cities. The officers are: Wm. R. Lyman, President; Henry A. Lesassier, Vice President; Isidore Newman, Treasurer, and A. A. Brinsmade, Secretary.

BROKERS.

FRANK A. LEE,
Stocks, Bonds and Mortgages,
—— 167 Common street.

TOWNSEND & LYMAN,
Stock, Exchange and Coin,
—— 138 Gravier street.

E. H. LEVY,
Coin, Stock and Note Broker. City and State Taxes settled. 128 Gravier street,

——

JOHN KLEIN & CO.,
Stock, Bonds, City and State Securities,
—— 31 Carondelet street.

TIM DOHERTY,
Stocks, Bonds and Mortgages,
25 Carondelet street.

HOTELS.

Carrollton Private Boarding House, C. F. Conrad proprietor. Delightfully situated at the Carrollton Gardens, and easy of access by the green cars leaving corner of Canal and Baronne streets.

Cassidy's Hotel, Nos. 172 and 174 Gravier street.

Conti Verandah Hotel, No 25 Conti, between Chartres and Decatur streets. Convenient to steamboats and city cars, being within three minutes walk of Canal street. Accommodations first class and terms reasonable. F. Bayha, (successor to Mrs. Schwarz,) proprietor.

City Hotel corner Camp and Common streets.

Louisiana Hotel, Nos. 213 and 215 Tchoupitoulas.

St. Charles Hotel, St. Charles, Gravier and Common streets.

St. James Hotel, Magazine, between Gravier and Natchez streets.

Waverly Hotel, corner Camp and Poydras, T. W. Kidder proprietor; European plan. Board $2 per day. Rooms from $4 to $6 per week. Lodging 50 to 75 cents per night. Only one square from the Galveston ticket office.

RESTAURANTS.

ANTOINE'S—No. 65 St. Louis street. Board by the day or week. Furnished rooms for boarders. Private saloons up stairs for weddings, baptisms, etc.

FOUR SEASONS' RESTAURANT—No. 111 Chartres street. Furnished rooms. Private saloons. Board and lodging $2 per day. Board by the week or month. J. Bosio proprietor.

DENECHAUD'S—No. 8 Carondelet street near Canal. Every delicacy of the market. Rooms for private and society dinners. Board by the week or month. E. F. Denechaud proprietor.

JOHN'S—Nos. 16 and 18 Bourbon street. Every accommodation of a first class house, and all the comforts and security of a home. .Elegantly furnished rooms fronting on Canal street connected with the restaurant. Meals at all hours. John Strenna proprietor.

VICTOR'S—Meals at all hours. Board by the day, week or month. Every accommodation of a first class restaurant. Elegantly furnished rooms for families. Nos. 38 and 40 Bourbon street, between Custom House and Bienville streets. Victor Bero, proprietor.

FRED'S—No. 106 St. Charles street, near St. Charles Theatre. Restaurant and lodging house. Open day and night. Meals at all hours at reasonable prices. J. F. Helmer & Co., proprietors.

McCLOSKEY'S—Nos. 70 and 72 St. Charles street. The best the market affords at prices to suit the times. Rooms for private and society dinners. Richard McCloskey, proprietor.

MAGNOLIA—Restaurant and oyster saloon. No. 95 St. Charles street. Meals 50 cents, served at all hours. Board $5 per week and meals from 6 A. M. to 9 P. M. Table best the market affords. On ball and gala nights open all night. Jacob Detzel, proprietor.

COSMOPOLITAN—13 and 15 Royal street. House newly refitted. Meals at all hours. Table supplied with the choicest of the market. Board and lodging $2 50 per day Weddings and parties attended to. Louis Chaplain, proprietor.

HOSPITALS.

CHARITY HOSPITAL.

The history and character of this admirable institution are closely connected with those of New Orleans from its infancy.

The Charity Hospital was founded in the year 1786 by the great and good Don Andros Almonoster y Roxas, through whose generosity it was supported for many years.

In 1815 the old Charity Hospital was built on the square now occupied by the Law and Medical Departments of the University, where it remained till 1832, when the present large and commodious building was erected. The buildings and grounds occupy two squares, bounded by Common, Howard, Gravier and Freret streets.

When we say that the general management of this institution is, and has been for many years, confided to that most exalted order of the Catholic Church, the Sisters of Charity, we need hardly add that the domestic arrangements of the hospital are perfect and satisfactory. The Medical Schools are allowed the use of the hospital for clinical teaching. The resident officers are Andrew Smythe, M. D , House Surgeon ; J. A. Root, Assistant House Surgeon. There are also several resident students.

MARINE HOSPITAL.

This very large, commodious building, situated on Common, near Broad, is built of iron but is not quite completed. It was used for several years as a hospital for negroes.

In addition to the Charity and Marine Hospitals, there are several private hospitals in the city, of which the following are the most important :

HOTEL DIEU, Corner Common and Galvez streets.

CIRCUS STREET INFIRMARY, Rampart, near Poydras.

TOURO INFIRMARY, New Levee and Gaiennie.

CEMETERIES.

Owing to the extreme moisture of the ground in and around the city, all excavations beyond two or three feet in depth are soon filled with water. On this account it is not practicable to bury under the ground in most localities, and the dead are, therefore, generally enclosed in vaults or tombs.

We do not think it necessary to give a list of all the cemeteries and their locations, but will refer strangers to those containing tombs which are objects of general interest.

WASHINGTON CEMETERY,

corner of Prytania street and Washington avenue, contains many beautiful souvenirs of the Confederate dead, and the monument erected *by the people* of Louisiana in memory of their last Governor, who filled the executive chair, HENRY W. ALLEN.

FIREMEN'S,

One of the Metaire Ridge Cemeteries, at the end of Canal street. Monument of Irad Ferry, the first fireman of this city who was killed while discharging his duty at a fire; society tombs of many of the fire companies, and other beautiful crypts.

GREENWOOD,

At the end of Canal street. Here is located the Confederate Monument, erected by the ladies of New Orleans in memory of the

"Braves who fought and fell."

A magnificent work of love, which the sculptor has aided by his finest efforts.

METAIRIE RIDGE,

At the head of Canal street, across the canal. This burial ground has but lately been laid out, yet contains many fine tombs, and splendid walks and drives.

OLD ST. LOUIS,

Between Conti and St. Louis streets. The burial ground of our oldest creole families, contains many beautiful tombs. Oldest cemetery in the city.

ST. LOUIS, 1, 2 AND 3,

Between Custom House and St. Louis streets. Contains some magnificent mausoleums. No. 2 holds the monument of John Milne, "The friend of the Orphan." No. 1 is exclusively for colored persons.

The Protestant Episcopal, (Girod street,) at the foot of Girod street, on Liberty. The oldest Protestant burial ground in the city. Has many fine tombs.

UNIVERSITY OF LOUISIANA.

Only the Medical and Law Departments of the University have been put in operation. The former was founded in 1834, under the title of the Medical College of Louisiana; but, in 1845, the success and fame of the College induced the State Convention to establish by the Constitution a University in New Orleans, and to constitute the Medical College as then organized the Medical Department of the University. The founders of the College, who also constituted its first faculty, were:

Dr. Thomas Hunt, Professor of Anatomy and Physiology; Dr. John Harrison, Adjunct—Demonstrations in Anatomy by—Dr. Chas. A. Luzenburg, Professor of Surgery; Dr. J. Munroe Mackie, Professor of Practice; Dr. T. Ingalls, Professor of Chemistry; Dr. Aug. H. Cenas, Professor of Midwifery; Dr. E. Bathurst Smith, Professor of Materia Medica.

Professor Hunt, the Dean, delivered the first introductory lecture in the presence of the friends of the undertaking and a few medical students. At the close of the first session eleven students had matriculated, which was deemed a cause of congratulation. During the first session, Dr. Harrison was unable, on account of personal sickness, to perform his duties, and Dr. Warren Stone demonstrated anatomy. Dr. E. H. Barton was substituted for Dr. Smith, who withdrew from the faculty before the session began. Of these nine gentlemen only Dr. Cenas is yet living.

By means of appropriations made by the State from time to time, the institution is furnished with all the appliances necessary for thorough courses of instruction in all the branches of medicine. Its Museum contains the only complete set, in this country, of wax models, from the Academy of Anatomy at Florence, and has been recently enriched by valuable additions in comparative anatomy and American archœology from the collections of Professor Joseph Jones, M. D.

The three buildings belonging to the two departments occupy the entire front on the south side of Common street, between Baronne and Dryades, and form the handsomest group of public edifices in the city.

The present organization is as follows:

President of the University,

HON. RANDELL HUNT, LL.D.

Medical Faculty.

A. H. CENAS, M. D., Emeritus Professor of Obstetrics and Diseases ot Women bnd Children.

T. G. RICHARDSON, M. D., Professor of General and Clinical Surgery.

SAMUEL M. BEMISS, M. D., Professor of the Theory and Practice of Medicine and Clinical Medicine.

STANFORD E. CHAILLE, M. D., Professor of Physiology and Pathological Anatomy.

FRANK HAWTHORN, M. D., Professor of General and Clinical Obstetrics and Diseases of Women and Children.

JOSEPH JONES, M. D., Professor of Chemistry and Clinical Medicine.

SAMUEL LOGAN, M. D., Professor of Anatomy and Clinical Surgery.

ERNEST S. LEWIS, M. D., Professor of Materia Medica and Therapeutics and Clinical Medicine.

Demonstrators of Anatomy.

EDMOND SOUCHON, M. D., ALBERT B. MILES, M. D.

Law Department.—Faculty.

RANDELL HUNT, LL. D., Professor of Constitutional Law, Commercial Law and the Law of Evidence.

CARLETON HUNT, Professor of Admiralty and International Law.

THOMAS ALLEN CLARKE, Professor of Common Law and Equity Jurisprudence.

THOMAS J. SEMMES, Professor of Civil Law.

www.ingramcontent.com/pod-product-compliance
Lightning Source LLC
LaVergne TN
LVHW050516100826
845148LV00002B/361

* 9 7 8 1 4 2 5 5 2 1 5 7 8 *